Stylish Jewelry
made simple

stringing • wirework • stitching

Kalmbach Books
21027 Crossroads Circle
Waukesha, Wisconsin 53186
www.Kalmbach.com/Books

© 2014 Kalmbach Books

All rights reserved. Except for brief excerpts for review, this book may not be reproduced in part or in whole by electronic means or otherwise without written permission of the publisher.

Photography © 2014 Kalmbach Books except where otherwise noted.

The jewelry designs in *Stylish Jewelry Made Simple* are the copyrighted property of the designer, and they may not be taught or sold without permission. Please use them for your education and personal enjoyment only.

Published in 2014
18 17 16 15 14   1 2 3 4 5

Manufactured in China

ISBN: 978-1-62700-079-6
EISBN: 978-1-62700-111-3

The material in this book has appeared previously in *Bead Style* magazine. *Bead Style* is registered as a trademark.

Editor: Erica Swanson
Art Director: Carole Ross
Illustrator: Kellie Jaeger
Photographers: James Forbes, William Zuback

Publisher's Cataloging-in-Publication Data
Stylish jewelry made simple : stringing, wirework, stitching / [compiled
  by Kalmbach Books] ; editor: Erica Swanson.

   pages : color illustrations ; cm

  At head of title: 45 chic projects
  "The material in this book has appeared previously in Bead Style magazine." —Title page verso.
  Issued also as an ebook.
  ISBN: 978-1-62700-079-6

  1. Beadwork—Handbooks, manuals, etc. 2. Beadwork—Patterns. 3. Wire jewelry—Handbooks, manuals, etc. 4. Jewelry making—Handbooks, manuals, etc. I. Swanson, Erica, editor. II. Kalmbach Publishing Company. III. Title: 45 chic projects IV. Title: BeadStyle magazine.

TT860 .S79 2014
745.594/2

CONTENTS

Introduction 4

Projects

REDS ●●●●●●●●●●
Golden ruby bracelets 6

Totally tubular cuff & earrings........................... 8

Vintage chic necklace & earrings..................... 10

Crystal kisses bracelet & earrings 13

Leather & luxe bracelet & earrings................... 16

GREENS ●●●●●●●●●●
Lush layers necklaces & earrings 20

Garden bracelet 23

Springtime sparkle necklace & earrings 25

Bountiful bangles & earrings................................ 28

Inspired by opposites necklace,
    bracelet, & earrings 30

Filigree forest necklace...................................... 34

Margarita mix necklace & earrings........................ 36

BLUES ●●●●●●●●●●
Easy gemstone necklace & earrings 40

Bubbly wire earrings.. 43

Clever kumihimo necklace 45

Prefab & pretty necklace & earrings 48

Crystal crests necklace & earrings 52

Charming links bracelet & earrings 55

Fab finishes necklace & earrings 58

PINKS ●●●●●●●●●●
Hugs & kisses bracelet & earrings 62

Leather & chain bracelet & earrings..................... 65

Stylish transfer pendant..................................... 67

Stick to pearls necklace & earrings 70

Flirty flower bangle 73

Lush loops necklace & earrings 75

NEUTRALS ●●●●●●●●●●
Textured three-strand necklace & earrings............ 79

Study in contrasts necklace,
    bracelet, & earrings 82

Breakout buttons bangles & earrings 86

Woven crystal and chain necklace & earrings....... 89

Pearl essence necklace & earrings 91

Keshi pearl necklace, bracelet, & earrings 94

Sail away bracelet 97

METALS ●●●●●●●●●●
Super hoop earrings 100

Marrakesh multistrand necklace & earrings 102

Poison pen earrings 105

Design on a dime bracelet & earrings.................. 107

Bridal wave necklace & cuff............................... 109

Grow fabulous flowers necklace & bracelet 112

Turning over new leaves necklace & earrings 115

MIXED ●●●●●●●●●●
Taffy garden necklace & earrings 119

Crescents of color necklace & earrings 122

Bohemian blooms necklace & earrings 125

A splash of color necklace 128

Bead bold necklace & earrings............................ 130

Charmed life necklace 133

Beader's Glossary 136

Basics 140

Contributors 142

Welcome to *Stylish Jewelry Made Simple*. The designs in this book, the best of the latest year of *Bead Style* magazine, are fresh and fun. Each project is a personal celebration of creativity. This book includes new materials, exciting color combinations, and, of course, new designs from some very creative people. Best of all, each project is clearly illustrated with complete step-by-step photos and instructions.

Stylish Jewelry Made Simple is organized by color, so you can pick the perfect shade to match your wardrobe. I'm sure you have a favorite, but I urge you to browse each category — you never know where you'll be inspired! We've included projects for beginners as well as more experienced beaders. There are pieces you can make in an hour or two, and some you could tackle in 15 minutes.

So, flip through the following pages, pick a project that excites you, and get started!

Let your creativity shine!

Naomi Fujimoto, Editor of *Bead Style*

"

I WANT TO BE DIFFERENT. IF EVERYONE IS WEARING BLACK, I WANT TO BE WEARING RED

-MARIA SHARAPOVA

"

Golden ruby
bracelets

When **Kelsey Lawler** turns to her stash and finds an abundance of ruby red, she can't always decide how best to use the beads — a memory wire cuff or a dangle bracelet? But why say "or" when you can say "and"? Both bracelets are perfect for using up your leftovers and can be adjusted according to the number of beads you have.

1 memory wire cuff • Use heavy-duty wire cutters to cut a piece of memory wire with the desired number of coils. Use roundnose pliers to make a loop on one end.

2 String beads and bead caps as desired (see note, below) until the bracelet is within ¼ in. (6 mm) of the finished length. Make a loop and trim the excess wire.

materials

memory wire cuff
- ◆ **14–18** 15 mm teardrop beads
- ◆ **20–26** 10–12 mm round beads
- ◆ **6–8** 8 mm rondelles
- ◆ **42–56** 4 mm round beads
- ◆ **20–26** 7 mm bead caps
- ◆ memory wire, 2½ in. (5 cm) diameter
- ◆ roundnose pliers
- ◆ heavy-duty wire cutters

dangle bracelet
- ◆ **10–12** 15 mm teardrop beads
- ◆ **8–10** 10–12 mm round beads
- ◆ **3–4** 8 mm rondelles
- ◆ **16–18** 3–4 mm round beads
- ◆ **10–12** 7 mm bead caps
- ◆ 5½–6½ in. (14–16.5 cm) chain, 4 mm links
- ◆ **21–26** 2-in. (5 cm) headpins
- ◆ **2** 4 mm jump rings
- ◆ lobster claw clasp
- ◆ 1 in. (2.5 cm) chain for extender, 6 mm links
- ◆ chainnose and roundnose pliers
- ◆ diagonal wire cutters

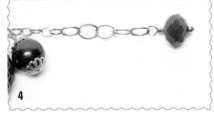

1 dangle bracelet • On a headpin, string one or two bead caps and beads as desired. Make the first half of a wrapped loop **(Basics)**. Make 21 to 26 bead units. Set one bead unit aside for step 4.

2 Cut a 5½–6½-in. (14–16.5 cm) piece of 4 mm link chain. Open a jump ring **(Basics)** and attach an end link and a lobster claw clasp. Close the jump ring.

3 Skip a few links and attach a bead unit. Complete the wraps. Attach a bead unit to every other link until the beaded section is within ½ in. (1.3 mm) of the finished length.

4 Use a jump ring to attach an end link and a 1-in. (2.5 cm) piece of 6 mm link chain. Attach a bead unit and the end link of the extender chain.

tips ●●●

No two stashes are the same, but consider this when stringing:

- • Keep to beads of a similar size.
- • Make one color dominant. For the cuff, I used two deep red beads for every light red one.
- • Use metal accents to tie the look together. In both bracelets, I used gold beads throughout and bead caps to frame the deep red pearls.

Totally tubular
cuff & earrings

For **Ashley Bunting,** the '80s live on in these colorful cuffs. Once you learn the (not very difficult) ladder stitch, you'll start dreaming of all the possibilities: neon brights, summery candy colors, even brushed metal. Try any bead with an elongated shape for a most excellent design.

1 bracelet • To make a toggle bar: Cut a 2-in. (5 cm) piece of wire. Make a small plain loop **(Basics)** on one end. String a 6–7 mm bead, an hourglass bead, and a 6–7 mm bead. Make a small plain loop.

2 Cut a 2-yd. (1.8 m) piece of waxed linen thread. Fold it in half. Place the narrowest part of a go-go pendant on top of the fold and bring both ends through the fold. Tighten the knot.

3 With one end, go around the go-go and through the loop. Tighten the knot.

4

5

6

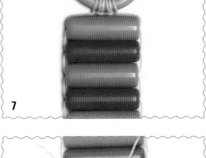

7

8

9

4 With the same end, repeat step 3.

5 With the other end, repeat step 3 twice.

6 On one end, string a tube bead. With the other end, go through the bead in the opposite direction.

7 Repeat step 6 with another tube. Continue stringing alternating

colors until the strand is within ¾ in. (1.9 cm) of the finished length.

8 About ¼ in. (6 mm) from the last bead, tie a surgeon's knot **(Basics)**.

9 Wrap each end in opposite directions around the center of the toggle bar two or three times. Tie a surgeon's knot and trim the excess thread.

1

2

1 **earrings •** For each earring: Open a jump ring **(Basics)**. Attach a 13 mm and a 35 mm ring. Close the jump ring.

2 Open the loop of an earring wire **(Basics)**. Attach the dangle and close the loop.

materials

bracelet
- ◆ 32 mm Lucite go-go pendant
- ◆ 21 mm Lucite hourglass bead
- ◆ **18–20** 28 mm Lucite tube beads, in two colors
- ◆ **2** 6–7 mm Lucite beads
- ◆ 2 yd. (1.8 m) waxed linen thread, 4 ply
- ◆ 2 in. (5 cm) 20-gauge wire
- ◆ chainnose and roundnose pliers
- ◆ diagonal wire cutters

earrings
- ◆ **2** 35 mm Lucite rings
- ◆ **2** 13 mm Lucite rings
- ◆ **2** 10 mm jump rings
- ◆ pair of earring wires with large loops
- ◆ **2** pairs of pliers

Beads from the Beadin' Path, beadingpath.com.

Vintage chic
necklace & earrings

Gay Isber works with a hoard of supplies that dates back to the 1940s–1980s, and this vintage, double-link chain is from her stash. Add crystals in warm copper tones to spice up the chain's matte finish.

components

connector • Cut a 1¾-in. (4.4 cm) piece of 20-gauge wire. Make a plain loop **(Basics)** on one end. String a graphic crystal and make a plain loop. Make 18 connectors.

cubist unit • Follow the instructions for the briolette unit, substituting a cubist pendant for the briolette.

briolette unit • Cut a 3½-in. (8.9 cm) piece of 22-gauge wire. With the tip of your roundnose pliers, make a small loop. In the opposite direction, make a medium-sized loop to make a figure 8.

String a briolette on the medium loop. Make a large loop around the small loop. Do not trim the excess wire. Make 10 briolette units.

6 On one side, open a jump ring (**Basics**) and attach the end links. Repeat on the other side. Check the fit, and trim chain if necessary.

7 Cut a 2-in. (5 cm) piece of 11–13 mm-link chain. On one end, attach the jump ring and chain. Attach a briolette unit and the end link. On the other end, use a jump ring to attach a clasp.

For the first strand: Open the loop of a connector (**Basics**). Attach the end link of a five-link chain and close the loop. Attach: connector, four-link chain, connector, three-link chain, connector. Cut a 3½–4½-in. (8.9–11.4 cm) and a 7–8-in. (18–20 cm) piece of chain. Attach the short chain and the first connector loop. Attach the long chain and the last loop.

2

1

necklace • Make the components (p. 10). Cut the following pieces of chain: one two-link, six three-link, five four-link, one five-link, one six-link.

5

For the fourth strand: Use six connectors to attach the following chains: three-link, two-link, six-link, four-link, three-link. Cut a 3–4-in. (7.6–10 cm) and a 10–11-in. (25–28 cm) piece of chain. Attach the short chain and the first connector loop. Attach the long chain and the last loop. Attach the cubist unit and the end link next to the last connector loop. Complete the wraps. Skipping a link, attach a briolette unit. Attach eight more briolette units, one to every fourth link, completing the wraps as you go.

3

For the second strand: Use three connectors to attach a four-link and a three-link chain. Cut a 5½–6½-in. (14–16.5 cm) and a 9–10-in. (23–25 cm) piece of chain. Attach the short chain and the first connector loop. Attach the long chain and the last loop.

4

For the third strand: Use five connectors to attach two four-link and two three-link chains. Cut a 4½–5½-in. (11.4–14 cm) and an 8½–9½-in. (21.6–24.1 cm) piece of chain. Attach the short chain and the first connector loop. Attach the long chain and the last loop.

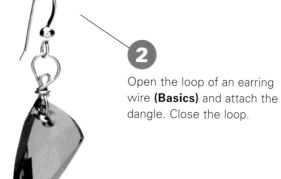

1

earrings • For each earring: Follow the instructions to make a briolette unit (p. 10), substituting an avant garde pendant for the briolette. Make the medium loop perpendicular to the small loop. Complete the wraps.

2

Open the loop of an earring wire **(Basics)** and attach the dangle. Close the loop.

note ●●●

The 11 mm crystal briolettes are Celestial Crystal drops in gold; the cubist, graphic, and avant garde crystals are Swarovski Elements in crystal copper.

materials

necklace 18–29 in. (46–74 cm)

- 22 mm cubist crystal pendant
- **18** 18 mm graphic crystals
- **10** 9–11 mm crystal briolettes
- 5½–7 ft. (1.7–2.1 m) chain, 7–8 mm links
- 2 in. (5 cm) chain, 11–13 mm links
- 32 in. (81 cm) 20-gauge wire
- 39 in. (99 cm) 22-gauge wire
- **2** 9–10 mm jump rings
- lobster claw clasp
- chainnose and roundnose pliers
- diagonal wire cutters

earrings

- **2** 20 mm avant garde crystal pendants
- 7 in. (18 cm) 22-gauge wire
- pair of earring wires
- chainnose and roundnose pliers
- diagonal wire cutters

Crystal kisses
bracelet & earrings

Embrace your sparkle with **Anna Elizabeth Draeger's** easy woven bracelet and earrings. The double layer of similar orange tones is all about heat. You can make larger versions of the bracelet and earrings by using 4 mm bicones and 11º seed beads.

1

2

3

4

5

6

materials

bracelet

- **210–248** 3 mm bicone crystals, **106–126** color A, **104–122** color B
- 5 g 15º seed beads
- flexible beading wire, .010
- **2** 7 mm jump rings
- crimp bead
- toggle clasp
- **2** pairs of pliers
- diagonal wire cutters
- crimping pliers (optional)

earrings

- **16** 3 mm bicone crystals, 8 color A, 8 color B
- **14** 15º seed beads
- beading thread
- **2** 7 mm jump rings
- pair of marquise earring wires
- **2** pairs of pliers
- beading needle
- scissors

1 bracelet • To make the color A strand: Cut a 3-ft. (91 cm) piece of beading wire. Center eight 15º seed beads. String one end through the eighth bead in the opposite direction. Go through all the beads again to reinforce the ring.

2 On each end, string a color A bicone crystal, a 15º, and an A. On one end, string a 15º.

3a String the other end through the last 15º in the opposite direction.

b Repeat steps 2 and 3a until the bracelet is within 1 in. (2.5 cm) of the finished length.

4a Cut a 3-ft. (91 cm) piece of beading wire. Center the eighth 15º in the ring from step 1.

b On each end, string the next A and 15º.

c String a color B bicone, a 15º, and a B. String the next 15º on the color A strand.

5 On each end, string a B. On one end, string a 15º and string the other end through in the opposite direction.

6a On each end, string a B and the next 15º on the A strand.

b Repeat steps 4c to 6a until you reach the end of the A strand.

note ●●●

The pieces use sun (A) and padparadscha champagne (B) crystals.

tip ●●●

The green dots in the photos for steps 4 and 6 indicate the beads you are exiting and the path you follow to create the bracelet.

7

8

7 Over each pair of wires, string three 15ºs.

8 On one pair of wires, string a crimp bead. String the other pair through in the opposite direction. Tighten the wires and crimp the crimp bead **(Basics)**. Trim the excess wire.

9 On each end, open a jump ring **(Basics)**. Attach half of a toggle clasp. Close the jump ring.

9

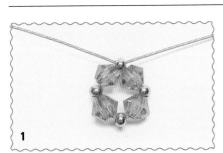

1

2

3

1 **earrings** • For each earring: Cut a 6-in. (15 cm) piece of beading thread. On the thread, center an alternating pattern of four color A bicone crystals and four 15ºs. Tie a surgeon's knot **(Basics)**. String one end through the adjacent 15º.

2 On one end, string a color B bicone, a 15º, and a B. On the other end, string a B, a 15º, a B, and a 15º. Tie a surgeon's knot. String the ends back through the adjacent beads and trim the excess thread.

3 Open a jump ring **(Basics)**. Attach the dangle and an earring wire. Close the jump ring.

Leather & luxe
bracelet & earrings

When making these bracelets, **Sarah Arnett** adapts the two-thread weave used by Chan Luu in her bracelets to capture pearls, squaredelles, and crystal-encrusted Bead Thru components with leather cord. The simple ladder stitch is a great way to combine classy and casual.

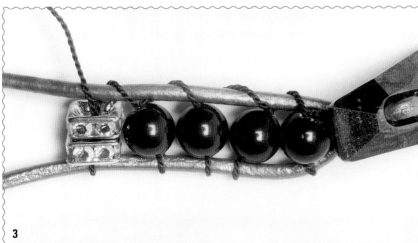

1 bracelet • Cut a 40–44-in. (1–1.1 m) piece of leather cord. Center a crystal button on the cord. Unwind the silk cord from the card. Next to the button, use a surgeon's knot **(Basics)** to tie the end of the silk cord around the leather cords. Trim the excess silk cord.

2 On the silk cord, string a pearl. Go around one leather cord and back through the pearl.

3a Bring the silk around the other leather cord and repeat step 2.
b Repeat steps 2 and 3a with two more pearls and a pair of squaredelles.

4 String each hole of a Bead Thru bar. Continue attaching pearls, squaredelles, and Bead Thrus (tip, right) until you can wrap the bracelet twice around your wrist.

5 Use a surgeon's knot to tie the silk cord around one leather cord. Tie both leather cords and the silk cord together in an overhand knot. Trim the excess silk cord. About ½ in. (1.3 cm) from the first knot, tie another overhand knot **(Basics)** with both leather cords. About ½ in. (1.3 cm) from the second knot, tie a third. Trim the cords, leaving ¾-in. (1.9 cm) tails.

materials

bracelet
- 17 mm trapeze crystal button
- **26–30** 6 mm round pearls
- **8** 6 mm squaredelles
- **4** 38 mm Bead Thru bars
- 40–44 in. (1–1.1 m) 1.5 mm leather cord
- card of silk bead cord, size 4 or 5
- scissors

earrings
- **4** 6 mm round pearls
- **2** 6 mm squaredelles
- **2** 1½-in. (3.8 cm) headpins
- pair of earring wires
- chainnose and roundnose pliers
- diagonal wire cutters

Supplies from Too Cute Beads, toocutebeads.com, or Fancy Beads, fancybeads.com.

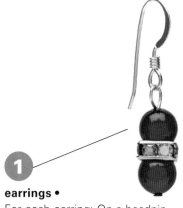

① earrings •
For each earring: On a headpin, string a pearl, a squaredelle, and a pearl. Make a plain loop **(Basics)**.

② Open the loop of an earring wire **(Basics)**. Attach the bead unit and close the loop.

tip ●●●

Depending on your wrist size, you may have to alter the placement of the beads. The Bead Thru bars should be across your wrist when the bracelet is wrapped.

The bracelet's mix of textures — leather, silk, pearls, metal, faceted crystal — is irresistible.

"
IT'S NOT EASY
BEING
GREEN

-KERMIT THE FROG
"

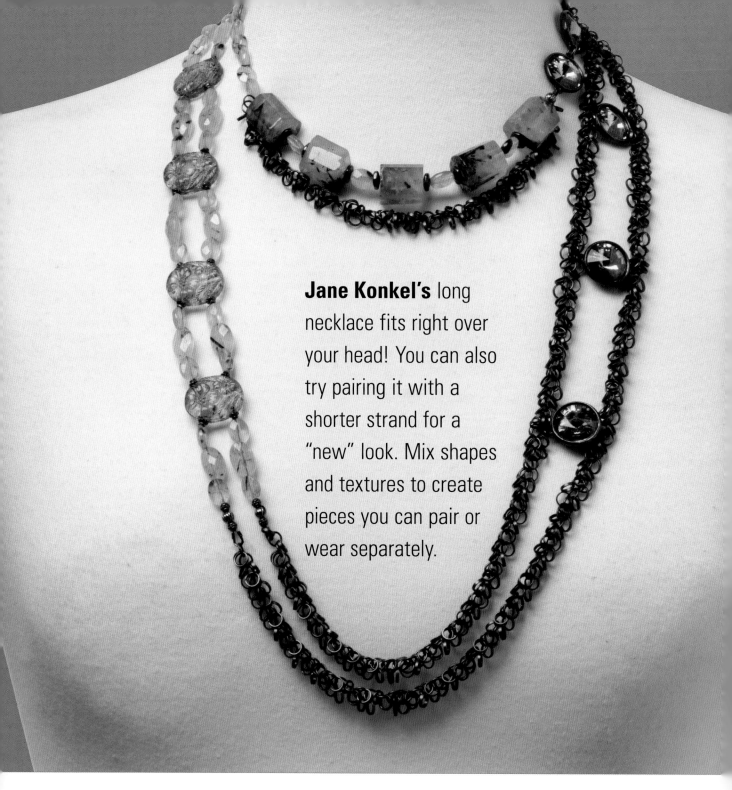

Jane Konkel's long necklace fits right over your head! You can also try pairing it with a shorter strand for a "new" look. Mix shapes and textures to create pieces you can pair or wear separately.

Lush layers
necklaces & earrings

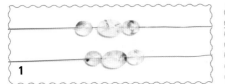

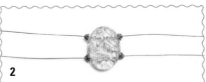

1 **long necklace • a** Cut two 16-in. (41 cm) pieces of beading wire. Cut an 18–20-in. (46–51 cm) and a 19–21-in. (48–53 cm) piece of chain.

b On each wire, string an 8 mm oval bead, a 12 mm oval, and an 8 mm.

2 **a** On each wire, string a 2.5 mm bead cap. Over both ends, string a double-drilled bead. On each end, string a bead cap.

b Repeat steps 1b and 2a three times. Repeat step 1b.

3 On one end, string: spacer, crimp bead, spacer, Wire Guardian, end link of an 18–20-in. (46–51 cm) chain. Repeat with the other wire. Go back through the last few beads strung and

tighten the wires. Attach the chains to the remaining ends. Crimp the crimp beads **(Basics)** and trim the excess wire. Close a crimp cover over each crimp.

4 **a** Apply glue to a link and place a rivoli in the link. Allow to dry. Make three or four links.

b About 6½ in. (16.5 cm) from one end of the chains, open a jump ring **(Basics)** and attach a loop of a rivoli link and a chain link. Close the jump ring.

5 Use a jump ring to attach the link's other loop and a link of the other chain. Use jump rings to attach the remaining links, spacing them about 2½ in. (6.4 cm) apart.

note ●●●

When designing pieces to layer, try combining gemstones, double-drilled beads, and rivolis in the same hue throughout each. Gunmetal is a fit companion to play up the dark inclusions in prehnite gemstones.

1 **short necklace •** Follow step 4a of the long necklace to make three rivoli links. Open a jump ring **(Basics)** and attach two links. Close the jump ring. Use a jump ring to attach another link.

Cut a 16-in. (41 cm) and a 10-in. (25 cm) piece of beading wire. On each wire, string a crimp bead, a Wire Guardian, and the loop of a rivoli link. Go back through the crimp bead and tighten the wire. Crimp the crimp bead **(Basics)** and trim the excess wire.

2 Cut a 6–8-in. (15–20 cm) piece of chain. On the long wire, string: end

link, round spacer, flat spacer, nugget, flat spacer, 8 mm oval bead.

3 String: flat spacer, nugget, flat spacer, 8 mm oval. Repeat twice. String a flat spacer, a nugget, a flat spacer, and the remaining end link.

4 On each wire, string: round spacer, five 8 mm ovals, bead cap, 12 mm oval, bead cap. String 8 mm ovals

until the strand is within 1 in. (2.5 cm) of the finished length.

5 On each end, string a round spacer, a crimp bead, and half of a magnetic clasp. Check the fit and add or remove beads if necessary. Go back through the last few beads strung, tighten the wire, and crimp the crimp bead. Trim the excess wire. Close a crimp cover over each crimp.

1 **leaf earrings** • For each earring: Cut a 3-in. (7.6 cm) piece of wire. Make the first half of a wrapped loop **(Basics)**. Attach a leaf pendant and complete the wraps.

2 String a bead cap, an oval bead, and a bead cap. Make a wrapped loop perpendicular to the first loop.

3 Open the loop of a lever-back earring wire **(Basics)** and attach the dangle. Close the loop.

materials

long necklace 28 in. (71 cm)
- **4** 20 mm double-drilled beads
- **3–4** 14 mm rivoli crystals
- **3–4** 14 mm rivoli links
- **10** 12 mm faceted oval gemstone beads
- **20** 8 mm faceted oval gemstone beads
- **8** 3 mm spacers
- **16** 2.5 mm bead caps
- flexible beading wire, .014 or .015
- **37–41** in. (.94–1 m) decorative circle chain
- **6–8** 6 mm jump rings
- **4** crimp beads
- **4** crimp covers
- **4** Wire Guardians
- **2** pairs of chainnose or bentnose pliers

- diagonal wire cutters
- G-S Hypo Cement
- crimping pliers (optional)

short necklace 16 in. (41 cm)
- **5** 15 mm gemstone nuggets
- **3** 14 mm rivoli crystals
- **3** 14 mm rivoli links
- **2** 12 mm faceted oval gemstone beads
- **22–32** 8 mm faceted oval gemstone beads
- **10** 6 mm flat spacers
- **5** 3 mm round spacers
- **4** 2.5 mm bead caps
- flexible beading wire, .014 or .015
- **6–8** in. (15–20 cm) decorative circle chain
- **2** 6 mm jump rings

- **4** crimp beads
- **4** crimp covers
- **2** Wire Guardians
- **2** pairs of chainnose or bentnose pliers
- diagonal wire cutters
- G-S Hypo Cement
- crimping pliers (optional)

leaf earrings
- **2** 54 mm filigree leaf pendants
- **2** 8 mm faceted oval gemstone beads
- **4** 2.5 mm bead caps
- 6 in. (15 cm) 22-gauge wire
- pair of lever-back earring wires
- chainnose and roundnose pliers
- diagonal wire cutters

Gemstones from Dakota Stones, dakotastones.com. Chain and leaf pendants from Beadaholique, beadaholique.com.

Garden
bracelet

Christi Friesen offers a fun and novice-friendly foray into the world of polymer clay. Mix clays and sculpt tiny leaves and moss for greenery, then add flower beads to bezels to plant miniature gardens. With a needle tool and your imagination, the sky's the limit to growing these colorful flower boxes!

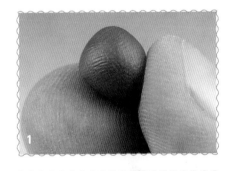

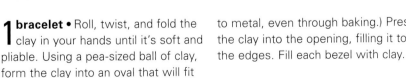

1 bracelet • Roll, twist, and fold the clay in your hands until it's soft and pliable. Using a pea-sized ball of clay, form the clay into an oval that will fit the opening of a bracelet bezel.

2 Apply glue to the bezel opening. (Poly Bonder glue adheres raw clay to metal, even through baking.) Press the clay into the opening, filling it to the edges. Fill each bezel with clay.

3 To make a flower unit: On a headpin, string a crystal (optional) and one or two flower beads. Use roundnose pliers to make a small hook. Trim the excess wire. Make one or two flower units per bezel.

4 Push a flower unit firmly into the clay. It may be helpful to first add a tiny ball of clay where the hook will go; it adds thickness for embedding the hook, but won't be noticeable.

5 Roll out a bit of clay. Using your fingers, form it into a leaf. Flatten the leaf. Make 10–20 leaves.

6 Using a needle tool or sculpting tool, gently press each leaf into the clay, being careful not to smash it.

7 Cut a 1-in. (2.5 cm) piece of wire. Center a dagger bead and twist the ends together. Use roundnose pliers to make a small hook. Trim the excess wire. Make 6–10 dagger units. Press the dagger units into the clay.

8 Using a needle tool or sculpting tool, swirl and scribble on the surface of the clay. Don't worry about the bits of clay; they add to the mossy texture.

9 Review the arrangement of bead units and leaves. Preheat the oven to 275° F (135° C). Fold a piece of parchment paper and place it over the bracelet, making sure it doesn't touch. Bake the bracelet for 30–45 minutes. Let it cool completely.

10 Optional: To add a patina, apply brown acrylic paint to the cracks and details in each garden. Use a damp sponge to remove paint from the surface of the clay.

note ●●●

Create pendants by filling single bezels with polymer clay. Include decorative headpins, pearls, or flower-shaped crystals to add dimension. If you make earrings, don't forget to make bezels that are mirror images of each other.

materials

bracelet
- 3 2-oz. (57 g) packages Premo Sculpey clay, in green shades
- 10–15 8–10 mm flower beads
- 6–10 8–12 mm dagger beads
- 2–5 3–4 mm bicone crystals
- bracelet blank with bezels
- 6–15 in. (15–38 cm) 28-gauge wire
- 5–10 1-in. (2.5 cm) decorative headpins
- chainnose and roundnose pliers
- diagonal wire cutters
- needle tool or sculpting tool
- Lisa Pavelka Poly Bonder glue
- parchment paper
- brown acrylic paint (optional)
- paintbrush (optional)
- sponge (optional)
- toaster oven or conventional oven

Bracelet blank (Patera bracelet with small ovals) from Nunn Design, nunndesign.com.

Springtime sparkle
necklace & earrings

Gorgeous and glitzy, cup chain isn't the first thing you'd think of for an everyday necklace. But **Naomi Fujimoto** pairs it with not-so-high-end howlite beads to make it fun and casual. Plus, finishing couldn't be easier with this new wire-wrapping technique.

1

2

3

4

5

6

7

8

9

10

1 necklace • To make a bead unit: Cut a 5-in. (13 cm) piece of wire. Center a teardrop bead and cross the wires above the bead.

2 About ¼ in. (6 mm) above the bead, grasp the wires with chainnose pliers. Bend each wire around the jaw.

3 Remove the pliers. Use your fingers to fold down each wire. Make seven bead units.

4 Cut a 14–16-in. (36–41 cm) piece of cup chain with an odd number of cups. Place each wire of the largest bead unit on each side of the center cup. Wrap the wires in opposite directions above the bead to complete the wraps. Trim the excess wire.

5 On each side, skipping a cup, attach a bead unit and the chain. Attach the remaining bead units and the chain. Check the fit, allowing 1 in. (2.5 cm) for finishing. Trim chain if necessary.

6 Cut a 10-in. (25 cm) piece of wire. On one end of the cup chain, center the wire and wrap it around the chain between the last two cups.

7 Wrap each end around the perimeter of the end cup twice.

8 With both wires, make the first half of a wrapped loop **(Basics)**. On the other end, repeat steps 6 and 7. Make the first half of a wrapped loop.

9 On one end, attach a lobster claw clasp and complete the wraps. Repeat on the other end, substituting a 1½-in. (3.8 cm) piece of cable chain for the clasp.

10 Cut a cup from a cup chain. Glue the cup to a metal tag. Allow to dry. Open a jump ring **(Basics)** and attach the tag and the end link. Close the jump ring.

tip ●●●

No end caps are necessary to finish this cup chain: Simply use wire to make a wrapped loop and attach a clasp!

materials

necklace 15 in. (38 cm)

- ◆ **7** 25–35 mm teardrop beads, top drilled
- ◆ 14½–15½ in. (36.8–41.9 cm) cup chain, 6 mm crystals
- ◆ 1½ in. (3.8 cm) cable chain, 8–9 mm links
- ◆ 7–9 mm metal tag
- ◆ 55 in. (1.5 m) 26-gauge wire
- ◆ 5–6 mm jump ring
- ◆ lobster claw clasp
- ◆ chainnose and roundnose pliers
- ◆ diagonal wire cutters
- ◆ G-S Hypo Cement

earrings

- ◆ **2** 25 mm teardrop beads, top drilled
- ◆ 2 cups from cup chain, 6 mm crystals
- ◆ 24 in. (61 cm) 26-gauge wire
- ◆ pair of earring wires
- ◆ chainnose and roundnose pliers
- ◆ diagonal wire cutters

Teardrop beads from Wendy Jewelry Supplies, wendyjewelry supplies.etsy.com.

1

2

3

4

5

6

1 earrings • For each earring: Cut a 12-in. (30 cm) piece of wire. Center a teardrop bead and cross the wires above the bead.

2 Cut a cup from a cup chain. Center it above the teardrop and wrap each wire twice around the perimeter of the cup in opposite directions.

3 With both wires, make a wrapped loop **(Basics)**. Do not trim the excess wire.

4 String one wire through the hole in the back of the cup.

5 Wrap both wires until you reach the loop. Trim the excess wire.

6 Open the loop of an earring wire **(Basics)**. Attach the dangle and close the loop.

Bountiful
bangles & earrings

Once **Madelin Adriani Pratama** starts playing with aluminum wire, she doesn't want to stop — which is why she can't limit her wire wrapping to just a couple of bangles. Become a *more-is-better* kind of gal and make a forearm full of stylish, stunning sets!

1 **single bangle** • Leaving the 10-gauge wire on the roll, pull the end around a bracelet mandrel at a size slightly smaller than your wrist. Cut the wire.

2 Keeping the wire on the mandrel, hammer it, striking the ends a few extra times to flatten them.

3 Cut a 20–30-in. (51–76 cm) piece of 20-gauge wire. Center a bead and bend each side of the wire down.

Position the bead over the ends of the 10-gauge wire.

4 Wrap the 20-gauge wire in opposite directions three or four times around the 10-gauge wire.

5 Wrap both ends under and around the edges of the bead. Trim the wire and tuck the ends. Attach one to three more beads as desired.

materials

single bangle
- **1–4** 12–22 mm beads
- 10-gauge Artistic Wire
- 20-gauge Artistic Wire
- chainnose pliers
- diagonal wire cutters
- heavy-duty wire cutters
- bracelet mandrel
- hammer

earrings
- **2** 12–22 mm beads
- 10-gauge Artistic Wire
- 10 in. (25 cm) 20-gauge Artistic Wire
- pair of earring wires
- chainnose and roundnose pliers
- diagonal wire cutters
- heavy-duty wire cutters
- hammer and bench block
- ring mandrel

1 **earrings •** Leave the 10-gauge wire on the roll and pull the end around a ring mandrel, making a loop large enough to accommodate a bead. Trim the end. Trim the stem to about 2 in. (5 cm).

2 Use roundnose pliers to curve the stem as desired. Make a loop at the end of the stem. Hammer the front side of the wire.

3 Cut a 5-in. (13 cm) piece of 20-gauge wire. Center a bead on the wire. Positioning the bead inside the large loop, wrap each end of the 20-gauge wire around the 10-gauge wire three or four times. Trim the excess wrapping wire and tuck the ends.

4 Open the loop of an earring wire **(Basics)**. Attach the dangle and close the loop. Make a second earring.

tip ●●●

To cut the 10-gauge wire, you can use memory-wire cutters or heavy-duty wire cutters.

note ●●●

Heavy beads tend to rotate to the inside of your wrist. To prevent this, attach a second bead as a counterweight to the opposite side of your bangle.

There's no limit to what you can do with wire!

Inspired by opposites
necklace, bracelet, & earrings

After figuring out how to place the focal point somewhere other than dead center, **Meredith Jensen** finds balance in contrary elements throughout her asymmetrical, multistrand necklace. The balance between calm and hyper colors, organic and polished stones, and a natural and elegant style mesh into a unified, fashionable design.

necklace • Cut a 19–23-in. (48–58 cm) piece of beading wire. Cut four more pieces, each 2 in. (5 cm) longer than the previous piece. On each wire, string 12 round beads (tip, below).

1

3

On each end, string: bead cap, spacer, 1¼ in. (3.2 cm) liquid silver beads, crimp bead, corresponding loop of a five-strand clasp (tip, p. 32). Check the fit, and add or remove beads if necessary. Go back through the beads just strung, tighten the wire, and crimp the crimp bead **(Basics)**. Trim the excess wire.

2

On the shortest wire, string a bead cap, ¾ in. (1.9 cm) of heishi beads, and a bead cap. String rounds until the strand is within 3 in. (7.6 cm) of the finished length. Repeat on the remaining wires, stringing each heishi section about ¼ in. (6 mm) longer than the previous one.

tip •••

If you use smaller or larger beads for these projects, you'll need to adjust the number of beads used in step 1.

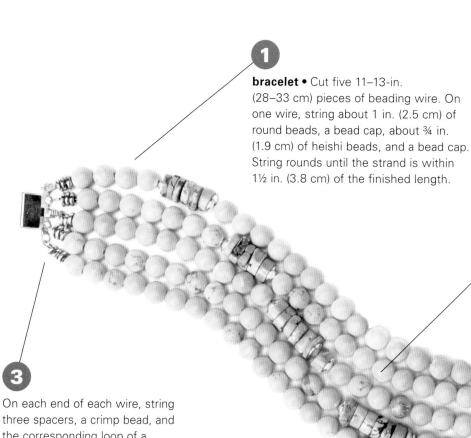

1

bracelet • Cut five 11–13-in. (28–33 cm) pieces of beading wire. On one wire, string about 1 in. (2.5 cm) of round beads, a bead cap, about ¾ in. (1.9 cm) of heishi beads, and a bead cap. String rounds until the strand is within 1½ in. (3.8 cm) of the finished length.

2

On each remaining wire, repeat the pattern in step 1, increasing the length of the first round-bead section on each strand.

3

On each end of each wire, string three spacers, a crimp bead, and the corresponding loop of a five-strand clasp (tip, below). Go back through the beads just strung, tighten the wire, and crimp the crimp bead **(Basics)**. Trim the excess wire.

tip

Before attaching the second end of each strand, close the clasp. This makes it easier to attach corresponding clasp loops and ensures that you don't overtighten the wires before crimping.

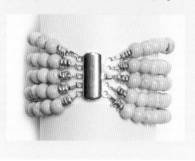

Design alternative
Try flipping the proportion of rondelles and round beads.

materials

necklace 20 in. (51 cm)

- 16-in. (41 cm) strand 7 mm heishi beads or rondelles
- **5** 16-in. (41 cm) strands 6 mm round beads
- 50–60 4–6 mm liquid silver beads
- **10** 2–4 mm spacers
- **20** 4 mm bead caps
- flexible beading wire, .014 or .015
- **10** crimp beads
- five-strand box clasp
- chainnose or crimping pliers
- diagonal wire cutters

bracelet

- **30–40** 7 mm heishi beads or rondelles
- **2** 16-in. (41 cm) strands 6 mm round beads
- **30** 4 mm flat spacers
- **10** 4 mm bead caps
- flexible beading wire, .014 or .015
- **10** crimp beads
- five-strand box clasp
- chainnose or crimping pliers
- diagonal wire cutters

earrings

- **10** 7 mm heishi beads or rondelles
- **6** 6 mm round beads
- **6** 4 mm flat spacers
- **10** 4 mm bead caps
- 8 in. (20 cm) 24-gauge wire
- **6** 2-in. (5 cm) headpins
- pair of earring wires
- chainnose and roundnose pliers
- diagonal wire cutters

1

2

3

4

1 **earrings** • For each earring: On a headpin, string a round bead and a bead cap. Make a wrapped loop **(Basics)**. Make three bead units.

2 Cut a 4-in. (10 cm) piece of wire. Make the first half of a wrapped loop. Attach each bead unit and complete the wraps.

3 String three spacers, a bead cap, five heishi beads, and a bead cap.

Make the first half a wrapped loop. Attach a soldered jump ring and complete the wraps, overlapping the excess wire.

4 Open the loop of an earring wire **(Basics)** and attach the dangle. Close the loop.

Filigree forest
necklace

A row of trees along **Jane Konkel's** necklace makes a big, green statement. Add metal beads and shimmering nylon chain to these lightweight pendants.

1

2

3

4

5

1 necklace • Open a 4 mm jump ring **(Basics)** and attach a pendant. Close the jump ring. Attach 4 mm jump rings to a total of five pendants. Cut a 12-in. (30 cm) piece of beading wire. Center a pendant on the wire.

2 On each end, string: flat spacer, tube bead, round spacer, flat spacer, enamel bead, flat spacer, round spacer, tube, flat spacer, pendant. Repeat.

3 On each end, string: flat spacer, tube, round spacer, flat spacer, enamel bead, flat spacer, round spacer, crimp bead, round spacer.

4 Cut two 4–6-in. (10–15 cm) pieces of nylon chain. On each end of the beaded strand, string an end link. Go back through the last few beads strung. Tighten the wire and crimp the crimp bead **(Basics)**. Trim the excess wire.

5 On each end, use an oval jump ring to attach half of a toggle clasp.

Design alternative

For a scaled-back necklace, attach just one tree pendant and a few nylon links to a long chain.

materials

necklace 17 in. (43 cm)
- **5** 48 mm filigree tree pendants
- **6** 6 mm enamel beads
- **10** 12 mm tube beads
- **22** 4 mm flat spacers
- **14** 3 mm round spacers
- flexible beading wire, .014 or .015
- 8–12 in. (20–30 cm) nylon chain, 11 mm links

- **2** 5 mm oval jump rings
- **5** 4 mm jump rings
- 2 crimp beads
- toggle clasp
- **2** pairs of pliers
- diagonal wire cutters
- crimping pliers (optional)

Enamel pendants and beads from Rings & Things, rings-things.com.

These beads make **Naomi Fujimoto** think of summer warmth. Combine chartreuse with fuchsia and green turquoise for a refreshing necklace any day of the year.

Margarita mix
necklace & earrings

1

2

3

4

5

1 necklace • Cut a 17-in. (43 cm) piece of beading wire. String a teardrop bead, a bicone crystal, a teardrop, and a round bead. Repeat the pattern until you've strung six or seven teardrops, ending with a teardrop.

2 Cut an 18-in. (46 cm) piece of beading wire. String a teardrop, a round, a teardrop, and a bicone. Repeat the pattern until you've strung seven or eight teardrops, ending with a teardrop.

3 On one side, on each end, string a crimp bead. String a jump ring over both ends and go back through the last few beads strung. Tighten the wire and crimp the crimp bead **(Basics)**. Trim the excess wire.

4 Fold a piece of ribbon in half to make a loop. On one side, string both ends through the jump ring. Go through the loop and tighten the knot. Repeat on the other side.

5 On each side, tie an overhand knot **(Basics)** with both ribbons, about 1 in. (2.5 cm) from the ends. To wear, tie the pairs of ribbons in a bow.

1

2

1 earrings • For each earring: Cut a 1¼-in. (3.2 cm) piece of wire. On one end, make a large plain loop **(Basics)**. String a bicone crystal and make a plain loop perpendicular to the first loop.

2 Open the large loop **(Basics)**. Attach a Lucite pendant and close the loop. Attach the dangle and the loop of an earring wire.

tip ●●●

Even though you can get by with one strand of teardrop beads, for just a few dollars more you can buy enough to be choosy and use only the prettiest pieces.

Design alternative

Dress up a simple strand with a brooch.

materials

necklace 16–22 in. (41–56 cm)

- ◆ **1 or 2** 15-in. (38 cm) strands 29 mm teardrop beads
- ◆ **5–7** 8 mm round beads
- ◆ **6** 8 mm bicone crystals
- ◆ flexible beading wire, .018 or .019
- ◆ **2** 36–40-in. (.9–1 m) silk ribbons, ½ in. (1.3 cm) wide
- ◆ **2** 7–9 mm soldered jump rings

- ◆ **4** crimp beads
- ◆ chainnose or crimping pliers
- ◆ diagonal wire cutters

earrings

- ◆ **2** 30–40 mm Lucite pendants
- ◆ **2** 8 mm bicone crystals
- ◆ 2½ in. (6.4 cm) 22-gauge wire
- ◆ pair of earring wires

- ◆ chainnose and roundnose pliers
- ◆ diagonal wire cutters

Teardrop beads from Happy Mango Beads, happymangobeads.com. Lucite pendants from The Beadin' Path, beadinpath.com.

"I THINK I HAVE SOMETHING TONIGHT THAT'S NOT QUITE CORRECT FOR EVENING WEAR. BLUE SUEDE SHOES

-ELVIS PRESLEY"

Easy gemstone
necklace & earrings

Adrianna Amato mixes a few chunky rondelles with crystals and chain for a necklace that's just the right blend of showy and elegant. Turquoise is one of her favorite materials to work with, but you can customize this look with any gemstone.

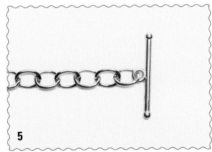

1 **necklace** • Cut a 14-in. (36 cm) piece of beading wire. String: crystal rondelle, spacer, bead cap, gemstone rondelle, bead cap, spacer. Repeat five times, then string a crystal rondelle.

2 Close two 5–6 mm jump rings **(Basics)**. On each end of the beaded strand, string a crimp bead and a jump ring. Go back through the last few beads strung and tighten the wire. Crimp the crimp bead **(Basics)** and trim the excess wire. If desired, close a crimp cover over the crimp.

3 Separate two individual 9 mm chain links as if opening a jump ring. Cut a 21–24-in. (53–61 cm) piece of 9 mm link chain. About 4 in. (10 cm) from each end of the chain, use a link to attach an end of the beaded strand and the 9 mm link chain. Close the link.

4 Cut an 11–13-in. (28–33 cm) and a 12–15-in. (30–38 cm) piece of 3 mm link chain. On each side, use a 4 mm jump ring to attach an end link of each 3 mm link chain and the 9 mm chain link where the beaded strand is attached.

5 Check the fit, allowing 1 in. (2.5 cm) for the clasp. Trim chain from each end if necessary. On each end, open the link and attach half of a toggle clasp. Close the link.

notes ●●●

• For faceted gemstone rondelles, try Carrie Gems, carriegems.etsy.com, Day Beads, daybeads.etsy.com, or Gemstone Universe, gemstoneuniverse.etsy.com. Many vendors sell loose beads (in addition to strands).

• For a subtle look, flatten the bead caps with nylon-jaw pliers before stringing the necklace.

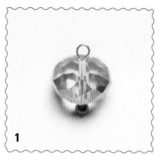

1 **earrings** • For each earring: On a headpin, string a round spacer and a crystal rondelle. Make a plain loop **(Basics)**.

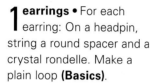

2 Cut a ¾-in. (1.9 cm) piece of chain. Open the loop of the bead unit **(Basics)** and attach an end link. Close the loop.

3 Open the loop of an earring wire. Attach the dangle and close the loop.

materials

necklace 17½–22 in. (44.5–56 cm)
- ◆ **6** 20 mm faceted gemstone rondelles
- ◆ **7** 14 mm crystal rondelles
- ◆ **12** 3 mm round spacers
- ◆ **12** 10 mm filigree bead caps
- ◆ flexible beading wire, .014 or .015
- ◆ 22–25 in. (56–64 cm) cable chain, 9 mm links
- ◆ 23–28 in. (58–71 cm) chain, 3 mm links
- ◆ **2** 5–6 mm jump rings
- ◆ **2** 4 mm jump rings
- ◆ **2** crimp beads
- ◆ toggle clasp
- ◆ **2** crimp covers (optional)
- ◆ chainnose or crimping pliers
- ◆ diagonal wire cutters

earrings
- ◆ **2** 12 mm crystal rondelles
- ◆ **2** 3 mm round spacers
- ◆ 1½ in. (3.8 cm) chain, 3 mm links
- ◆ **2** 1½-in. (3.8 cm) headpins
- ◆ pair of earring wires
- ◆ chainnose and roundnose pliers
- ◆ diagonal wire cutters

Bubbly wire earrings

Madelin Adriani Pratama's framed teardrops dangle from fancy handmade aluminum earring wires. Aluminum wire is perfect for earrings. It's lightweight and soft enough to texturize with a hammer, but sturdy enough to hold its shape. It comes in a variety of colors, is available at craft stores, and is inexpensive. It's a miracle metal!

1 earrings • To make a bead unit: On a headpin, string a bead and make a plain loop **(Basics)**. Make six bead units.

2 Cut a 12-in. (30 cm) piece of 20- or 22-gauge wire. Make a small loop on one end. Pull the wire around a 7 mm mandrel to form a circle. Pull the wire around a 6 mm mandrel in the opposite direction to form another circle.

3

4

5

6

7

8

9

10

11

12

3 Pull the wire around a 4 mm mandrel to form a circle. Pull the wire around roundnose pliers in the opposite direction to form another circle.

4 Pull the wire around the 4 mm mandrel to form a circle. Pull the wire around the 7 mm mandrel in the opposite direction to form another circle.

5 Pull the wire around roundnose pliers in the opposite direction to form a circle. On a bench block, lightly hammer each side.

Place the bottom of the piece against a 6 mm mandrel. Pull the wire halfway around the mandrel toward the top of the piece.

6 Place the top of the piece against an 8 mm mandrel. Pull the wire halfway around the mandrel toward the bottom of the piece. Trim the wire slightly below the bottom of the piece. Use chainnose pliers to bend the tip upward. Hammer the earring wire and file the end.

7 Open the loop of a bead unit **(Basics)** and attach a circle. Close the loop. Attach the remaining bead units to circles as desired.

8 To make the frame: Cut a 5-in. (13 cm) piece of 16-gauge wire. Wrap it around a teardrop bead.

9 Trim one end to ½ in. (1.3 cm). Use roundnose pliers to make a loop. Hammer the frame.

10 Cut a 6-in. (15 cm) piece of 24-gauge wire. Center the bead on the wire. Wrap each end around the frame three or four times. Trim the excess wire and tuck the ends.

11 Cut a 14-in. (36 cm) piece of 20- or 22-gauge wire. Starting at the loop, wrap the wire around the frame until you've covered the top third of the bead. Trim the excess wire and tuck the ends.

12 String the frame's loop on the earring wire. Make a second earring the mirror image of the first.

materials

earrings

- **2** 24 mm flat teardrop beads, top drilled
- **12** 3–6 mm beads
- 10 in. (25 cm) 16-gauge wire
- 52 in. (1.3 m) 20- or 22-gauge wire
- 12 in. (30 cm) 24-gauge wire
- **12** 1-in. (2.5 cm) headpins
- chainnose and roundnose pliers
- diagonal wire cutters
- hammer and bench block
- metal file or emery board
- 4, 6, 7, and 8 mm mandrels or a wire jig and pegs

Set of jump ring mandrels from Beadalon, beadalon.com for store locations.

Clever
kumihimo
necklace

Anne Dilker loves the look of delight when beaders realize just how simple and fun kumihimo is. If you've never done it before, this project is a perfect way to start. It's just one step beyond the basic braid, with beads added to a single cord.

materials

necklace 18 in. (46 cm)

- ◆ **130** 6º seed beads
- ◆ **3** 45-in. (1.4 m) pieces of #1 rattail
- ◆ 60-in. (1.5 m) piece of #18 S-Lon
- ◆ 8–10 in. (20–25 cm) chain, 10–12 mm links
- ◆ 4 in. (10 cm) 20–24-gauge wire
- ◆ **4** 8 mm jump rings
- ◆ **2** 5 mm end caps
- ◆ S-hook clasp
- ◆ kumihimo braiding disk
- ◆ **8** bobbins or pieces of cardboard
- ◆ big-eye beading needle
- ◆ chainnose and roundnose pliers
- ◆ diagonal wire cutters
- ◆ thread
- ◆ gel glue
- ◆ scissors
- ◆ weight

1 **necklace** • Center the rattail and S-Lon strands over the hole of a braiding disk. Position each cord in the notch on either side of two dots, creating an X with the pairs as shown. On each end of the S-Lon, string 65 6º seed beads. Wind each strand (also called a warp) on a bobbin or piece of cardboard.

2 Cut a 4-in. (10 cm) piece of 20–24-gauge wire. Make the first half of a large wrapped loop **(Basics)**. From the bottom of the braiding disk, attach the loop where the warps cross. Complete the wraps. Make the first half of a large wrapped loop. Attach a weight and complete the wraps.

3 To begin the braid, remove the top right warp, and bring it down to the notch next to the bottom right warp.

4 Remove the bottom left warp from the notch and bring it up to the notch next to the top left warp.

5 **a** Turn the braiding disk a ¼ turn and repeat steps 3 and 4.
b Repeat steps 3 to 5a until the braid is ¼ in. (6 mm).

6 Continue braiding. Each time you move the beaded warp, bring one bead into the center of the disk, just under the first warp it crosses over. Continue until the braid is about 10 in. (25 cm) or until you run out of beads.

7

8

9

7a Braid for another ¼ in. (6 mm).
b About 1 in. (2.5 cm) from the end of the braid, tie the ends together with an overhand knot **(Basics)**. Wrap a piece of thread tightly around the warps several times near the end of the braid. Tie a square knot.

c Cut the warp strands between the knot and the thread. On the other end, remove the weight and repeat step 7b over the doubled ends.

8 On each end, fill an end cap halfway with glue and insert the end of the braid. Allow to dry.

9 Cut two 3–4-in. (7.6–10 cm) chains. On each end, open a jump ring **(Basics)** and attach an end link and the loop of an end cap. Close the jump ring. On one end, use a jump ring to attach an S-hook clasp and an end link. Attach a jump ring to the remaining end link.

tips ●●●

- Instead of using four cords doubled, you can use eight shorter cords and tie them off (as in step 7) before attaching the weight.
- This project uses #18 S-Lon (also sold as Tex210 or C-Lon), but if you decide to use #1 (lightweight) rattail for your beaded strand, you can make stringing the 6ºs a little less challenging by applying glue to the end of the cord, letting it dry, and then trimming it into a point.
- The weight is attached to keep the braiding tension uniform. This project uses a stamp, but almost anything that can be attached with the wire will work (25 pennies in a plastic bag makes a good weight).

Design alternative

Changing the number and type of beads creates a variety of looks. Experiment to see what happens when you string various colors on the strands.

Prefab & pretty
necklace & earrings

With these gemstone chains and bezeled pendants, the tiny wrapped-looping and stone setting are already done for you! **Naomi Fujimoto's** necklace uses plain and wrapped loops to connect the elements, but you could just as easily do that with jump rings. All you need is a design idea — or many!

nugget strand

1 Cut a 3½-in. (8.9 cm) piece of 20-gauge wire. Make a wrapped loop **(Basics)**. String a faceted nugget and make a wrapped loop. Make seven to nine nugget units.

2 Open six to eight links of 8–9 mm link chain as you would a jump ring **(Basics)**. Attach a loop of a nugget unit and a loop of a second nugget unit. Close the link. Use links to attach the remaining nugget units.

wrapping chain

1 Cut two 4–5-in. (10–13 cm) pieces of 8–9 mm link chain. Open an end link of one piece. Attach an end link of a 3–5-ft. (.9–1.5 m) piece of 3 mm link chain, the nugget strand, and each gemstone chain. Close the end link.

2 Place one of the links of each 8–9 mm link chain on a peg of a Chain Sta. Wrap the remaining chains around the nuggets. Anchor them by going through the 8–9 mm links between nuggets and by wrapping the 3 mm link chain between nuggets.

3 When you reach the other end of the nugget strand, carefully open the 8–9 mm end link and attach each chain. If the loop of the gemstone chain is too small, use a 4 mm jump ring to attach it.

4 With all four chains, go back, wrapping until you reach the starting end. Attach the chains to the 8–9 mm end link and trim the excess chain.

2 On one end, use a 5–6 mm jump ring to attach an end link and a lobster claw clasp. Repeat on the other end, substituting a 2-in. (5 cm) piece of chain for the clasp.

3 On a headpin, string a crystal. Make the first half of a wrapped loop **(Basics)**. Attach the end link and complete the wraps.

chain-wrapped necklace •
Make a nugget strand and wrap the chain around it (p. 48).

1

On one end, use a jump ring to attach a lobster claw clasp and an end link. Repeat on the other end, substituting a 2-in. (5 cm) piece of 10–12 mm link chain for the clasp.

4

5

Repeat step 3 of the chain-wrapped necklace.

1

teardrop necklace •
On a headpin, string a metal bead. Make a plain loop **(Basics)**. Make six bead units.

On each side, use a jump ring to attach the next link and the loop of a bead unit. On the next links, attach a teardrop, a bead unit, a teardrop, and a bead unit.

3

2 Cut a 16–18-in. (41–46 cm) piece of 20–22 mm link chain with an odd number of links. Open a jump ring **(Basics)**. Attach a teardrop pendant and the center link. Close the jump ring.

1

2

3

4

materials

**chain-wrapped necklace
17 in. (43 cm)**

- **7–9** 25–35 mm faceted
  gemstone nuggets
- 25–32 in. (64–81 cm) 20-gauge
  wire
- 12–14 in. (30–36 cm) cable chain,
  8–9 mm links
- 8–12 ft. (2.4–3.7 m) gemstone
  chain, 4 mm rondelles, in
  three styles
- 3–5 ft. (.9–1.5 m) cable chain,
  3 mm links
- **2** 5–6 mm jump rings
- **1–12** 4 mm jump rings
- lobster claw clasp
- chainnose and roundnose pliers
- diagonal wire cutters
- Chain Sta (optional)

teardrop necklace 17 in. (43 cm)

- **5** 24–27 mm bezeled teardrop
  pendants
- **6** 20–23 mm metal beads
- 8 mm round crystal
- 16–18 in. (41–46 cm) chain,
  20–22 mm links
- **7** 1½-in. (3.8 cm) headpins
- **13** 5–6 mm jump rings
- lobster claw clasp
- 2 in. (5 cm) chain, 10–12 mm links
- chainnose and roundnose pliers
- diagonal wire cutters

tassel earrings

- 30–38 in. (76–97 cm) gemstone
  chain, 4 mm rondelles
- **2** cones
- 8 in. (20 cm) 24-gauge wire
- pair of earring wires
- chainnose and roundnose pliers
- diagonal wire cutters

*Gemstone chain and bezeled
pendants from Shivam Imports,
shivamimportsny.com. Supplies
also available from Etsy, etsy.com
(search "gemstone chain" and
"bezel chalcedony pendant" in
Craft Supplies).*

1 tassel earrings • For each earring:
Cut three or four 14–link pieces of
gemstone chain. Set aside one of the
rondelles from a cut link.

2 Cut a 4-in. (10 cm) piece of wire.
Make the first half of a wrapped
loop **(Basics)** on one end. Attach this
loop and the two center loops of each
chain. Complete the wraps.

3 String a cone and the rondelle from
step 1, and make a wrapped loop.

4 Open the loop of an earring wire
(Basics). Attach the dangle and
close the loop.

Crystal crests
necklace & earrings

This delicate piece reminds **Monica Han** of the movements of ocean waves. She can sit on the beach for hours watching and listening to the water — even the splashing has its own sound and rhythm. Recreate that feeling — the relaxing and re-energizing experience of the ocean — in this project.

components

1 long dangle • On a headpin, string a pear-shaped pearl. Make a wrapped loop **(Basics)**.

2 Cut a 3-in. (7.6 cm) piece of 22-gauge wire. Make the first half of a wrapped loop. String a round pearl and make the first half of a wrapped loop. Make three connectors.

3 On one loop of a connector, attach the pear-shaped unit. On the other loop, attach a second connector. Complete the wraps. Attach a third connector and complete the wraps.

1 wave dangles • Cut a 3½-in. (8.9 cm) piece of 22-gauge wire. Make the first half of a wrapped loop (tip, p. 54). Attach a 28 mm (large) wave pendant and complete the wraps.

2 String a 6 mm round pearl and make a wrapped loop. Make six large wave dangles and six 19 mm (small) wave dangles.

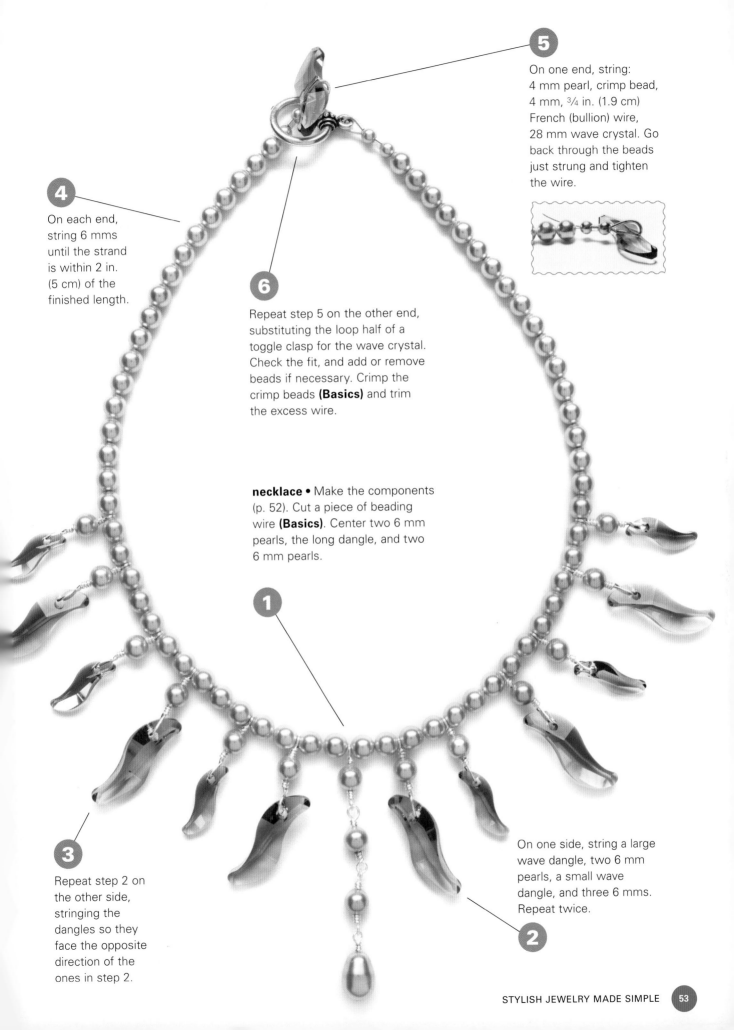

5

On one end, string:
4 mm pearl, crimp bead,
4 mm, ¾ in. (1.9 cm)
French (bullion) wire,
28 mm wave crystal. Go
back through the beads
just strung and tighten
the wire.

4

On each end,
string 6 mms
until the strand
is within 2 in.
(5 cm) of the
finished length.

6

Repeat step 5 on the other end,
substituting the loop half of a
toggle clasp for the wave crystal.
Check the fit, and add or remove
beads if necessary. Crimp the
crimp beads **(Basics)** and trim
the excess wire.

necklace • Make the components
(p. 52). Cut a piece of beading
wire **(Basics)**. Center two 6 mm
pearls, the long dangle, and two
6 mm pearls.

1

3

Repeat step 2 on
the other side,
stringing the
dangles so they
face the opposite
direction of the
ones in step 2.

2

On one side, string a large
wave dangle, two 6 mm
pearls, a small wave
dangle, and three 6 mms.
Repeat twice.

1

2

1 earring dangles • Cut a 5-in. (13 cm) piece of 22-gauge wire. Make the first half of a wrapped loop (**Basics**; tip, below). Attach a wave pendant and complete the wraps, extending them up the stem. Make a wrapped loop, extending the wraps down the stem. Make two long dangles.

2 Repeat step 1 with a 4-in. (10 cm) piece of wire. Make two short dangles.

earrings • For each earring: Make the earring dangles (above). Open a jump ring (**Basics**). Attach a long dangle, a short dangle, and the loop of an earring wire. Close the jump ring.

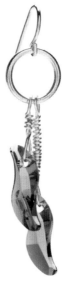

tip ●●●

Teardrop-shaped wrapped loops are a lot like round wrapped loops (**Basics**) but more suited to this shape of pendant. Use the jaw of your roundnose pliers to make a teardrop shape, then bend one end of the wire and make a set of wraps with the other.

materials

necklace 17 in. (43 cm)
- **6** 28 mm wave crystal pendants
- 28 mm wave crystal
- **6** 19 mm wave crystal pendants
- 11 mm pear-shaped crystal pearl
- 75–83 6 mm round crystal pearls
- **4** 4 mm round crystal pearls
- flexible beading wire, .014 or .015
- 51 in. (1.3 m) 22-gauge wire
- 1½-in. (3.8 cm) headpin
- **2** crimp beads
- French (bullion) wire
- 16 mm loop half of a toggle clasp
- chainnose and roundnose pliers
- diagonal wire cutters
- crimping pliers (optional)

earrings
- **4** 19 mm wave crystal pendants
- 18 in. (46 cm) 22-gauge wire
- **2** 12 mm jump rings
- pair of earring wires
- chainnose and roundnose pliers
- diagonal wire cutters

note ●●●

Monica used wave crystals in denim blue and pearls in light blue.

Charming links

bracelet & earrings

Crystal Clay studded with crystals is a beautiful look, but **Stephanie Gard Buss** has a different way to use the product. First, she bends a headpin into a grass shape. Then, she adds chatons to make the design blossom with buds and leaves.

components

1

2

note ●●●

Since the crystal color wasn't as close to the pearl color in the dark blue bracelet, I strung an extra crystal to keep the composition balanced.

1 **bead units** • Cut a 3-in. (7.6 cm) piece of wire. Make the first half of wrapped loop **(Basics)**. String a rondelle. Make the first half of a wrapped loop. Make three more bead units with 8–9 mm pearls. Make a fourth unit adding a bead cap to the pearl. Make a bead unit with a teardrop bead.

2 On a headpin, string an 8 mm round crystal. Make the first half of a wrapped loop.

tip ●●●

I used smaller (1.6 mm) chatons in this version so I could add a few extra without covering up too much of the black background.

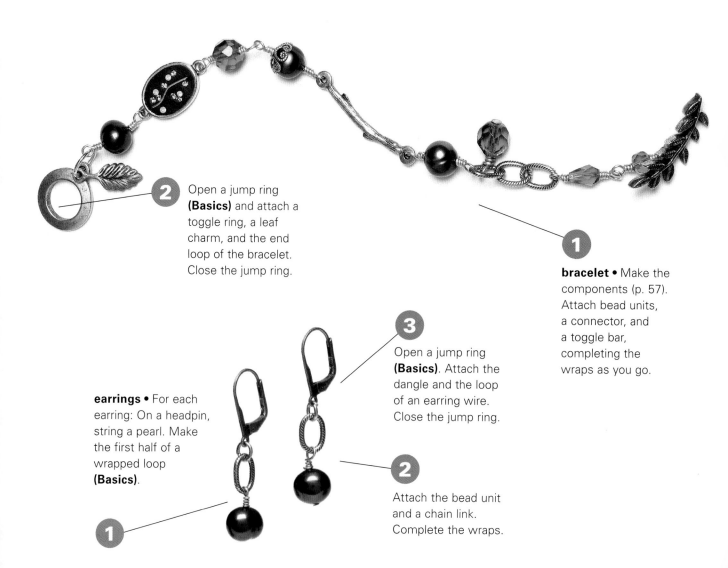

2 Open a jump ring **(Basics)** and attach a toggle ring, a leaf charm, and the end loop of the bracelet. Close the jump ring.

1 **bracelet** • Make the components (p. 57). Attach bead units, a connector, and a toggle bar, completing the wraps as you go.

3 Open a jump ring **(Basics)**. Attach the dangle and the loop of an earring wire. Close the jump ring.

earrings • For each earring: On a headpin, string a pearl. Make the first half of a wrapped loop **(Basics)**.

2 Attach the bead unit and a chain link. Complete the wraps.

1

components

1 **charm** • Measure equal amounts of two-part epoxy clay. You'll need about a pea-size amount of combined clay.

2 Use your fingers to mix the clay together for at least four minutes.

3 Fill a bezel with clay. The top should be level with the edge, not domed.

4 Cut a small wire "branch" and press it into the clay. Use a toothpick topped with a bit of putty or wax to pick up chatons and place them on the clay. Press them lightly into the clay with your finger. Allow the clay to cure on a flat surface for 24 hours.

tips •••

- Crystal Clay is pliable for about 90 minutes, so plan your design before adding the clay to the bezel.
- To remove fingerprints from the clay, wet your finger slightly and smooth the surface before it sets.

The manufacturer recommends the following safety tips: Keep the clay out of reach of children, work in a well-ventilated area, avoid touching your eyes while working, and wash your hands after use. If you have sensitive skin, consider wearing gloves.

materials

bracelet
- 4–5 8–9 mm potato pearls
- 8 mm round fire-polished crystal
- 8 mm fire-polished crystal teardrop
- 6 mm fire-polished crystal rondelle
- **6–10** 1.8 mm crystal chatons (PP 11)
- 14 mm oval bezel link with two loops
- 1-in. (2.5 cm) twig connector
- ³⁄₄-in. (1.9 cm) leaf charm
- 15 in. (38 cm) 22-gauge half-hard wire
- **3** 9 mm textured chain links
- 10 mm jump ring
- 1¹⁄₂-in. (3.8 cm) headpin
- 8 mm filigree bead cap
- leaf toggle bar
- toggle ring
- Crystal Clay (or other two-part epoxy clay), black chainnose and roundnose pliers
- diagonal wire cutters
- toothpick
- wax or putty

earrings
- **2** 8–9 mm potato pearls
- **2** 9 mm textured chain links
- **2** 1¹⁄₂-in. (3.8 cm) headpins
- **2** 4 mm jump rings
- pair of earring wires
- chainnose and roundnose pliers
- diagonal wire cutters

Visit Nunn Design, nunndesign.com, for retail information.

Fab finishes
necklace & earrings

Cathy Jakicic's necklace offers both texture and color. The speckled finish of the ceramic glaze combines with the earthy verdigris coating on the metal beads to give a monochromatic color palette a fascinating complexity.

adding patina to components

1 With a paintbrush, dab the brass metal coating on a clean jump ring. Let the first layer dry for 5–10 minutes and apply a second layer.

2 Apply a third layer of metal coating. While it's still wet, liberally brush on the verdigris patina. Set aside to let the color develop. The time it takes for the color to "bloom" will vary, but allow at least an hour to get the full effect. Allow the patinated components to dry for 72 hours. Apply sealant with a brush.

notes ●●●

- This project uses antiqued brass and brass findings, but the original colors were covered with the metal coating.
- If the surface of your piece is smooth, add texture with steel wool before applying the coating.

1

2

3

4

5

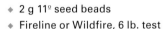

6

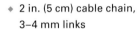

7

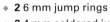

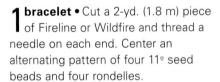

8

9

materials

bracelet

- ◆ **45–54** 6 mm fire-polished crystal rondelles
- ◆ **60–72** 3 mm fire-polished round crystals
- ◆ 2 g 11º seed beads
- ◆ Fireline or Wildfire, 6 lb. test
- ◆ 2 in. (5 cm) cable chain, 3–4 mm links
- ◆ **2** 6 mm jump rings
- ◆ **2** 4 mm soldered jump rings
- ◆ magnetic clasp
- ◆ 2 pairs of pliers
- ◆ scissors
- ◆ **2** #12 beading needles

earrings

- ◆ **8** 6 mm fire-polished crystal rondelles
- ◆ **4** 3 mm fire-polished round crystals
- ◆ **22** 11º seed beads
- ◆ Fireline or Wildfire, 6 lb. test
- ◆ **2** bead tips
- ◆ pair of earring wires
- ◆ chainnose pliers
- ◆ 2 pairs of pliers
- ◆ scissors
- ◆ G-S Hypo Cement

1 bracelet • Cut a 2-yd. (1.8 m) piece of Fireline or Wildfire and thread a needle on each end. Center an alternating pattern of four 11ºseed beads and four rondelles.

2 Go through the first rondelle so the threads exit in opposite directions. Tighten the thread.

3 On each end, string three 11ºs. On one end, string a 4 mm soldered jump ring.

4 With each end, go through the 11ºs on the other thread and the adjacent rondelle so the threads exit in opposite directions. Tighten the thread. Go through the 11ºs and the rondelle again to reinforce the loop.

5 On each end, string an 11º and a round crystal. Over both ends, string an 11º.

6 On each end, string a round crystal and an 11º. With each end, go through the rondelle so the threads exit in opposite directions. Tighten the thread.

7 With one end, string an alternating pattern of four 11ºs and three rondelles. Go back through the rondelle from step 6 so the threads exit in opposite directions. Tighten the thread.

8 Repeat steps 5, 6, and 7 until the strand is within 1 in. (2.5 cm) of the finished length. End with step 6.

9 Repeat steps 3 and 4. With one end, go through the 11ºs again so the threads are on the same side. Tie two overhand knots **(Basics)** and trim the excess thread.

10

11

10 On each end, open a 6 mm jump ring **(Basics)** and attach half of a clasp.

11 Cut a 2-in. (5 cm) piece of chain. On each end of the bracelet, attach the jump ring and an end link of chain. Close the jump ring.

tips •••

- Experiment with color and texture. Find a colorful picture that appeals to you and use those colors in a design.
- Use a variety of beads, seed bead sizes, and bead weaving techniques in a project to create texture.
- Enjoy the process. Save the pieces that aren't quite right; they may be the inspiration for a new project.

1

3

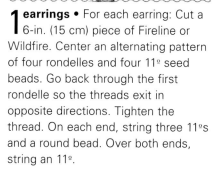

2

1 earrings • For each earring: Cut a 6-in. (15 cm) piece of Fireline or Wildfire. Center an alternating pattern of four rondelles and four 11º seed beads. Go back through the first rondelle so the threads exit in opposite directions. Tighten the thread. On each end, string three 11ºs and a round bead. Over both ends, string an 11º.

2 Over both ends, string an 11º and a bead tip. Tie two or three overhand knots **(Basics)** and trim the excess thread. Apply glue to the knots. Close the bead tip.

3 Use pliers to close the loop of the bead tip around the loop of the earring wire.

notes •••

- The beige Czech glass rondelles have extra color added in what is called a Picasso finish. The finish adds irregular touches of brown or green to the surface of the bead for a mottled look that sometimes resembles a gemstone.
- The lavender beads have a cathedral finish. There are a number of variations on the cathedral finish, but the term is used when the tips of the beads are coated with different colors — often metallics — or different textures. Cathedral beads are sometimes called windowpane beads.

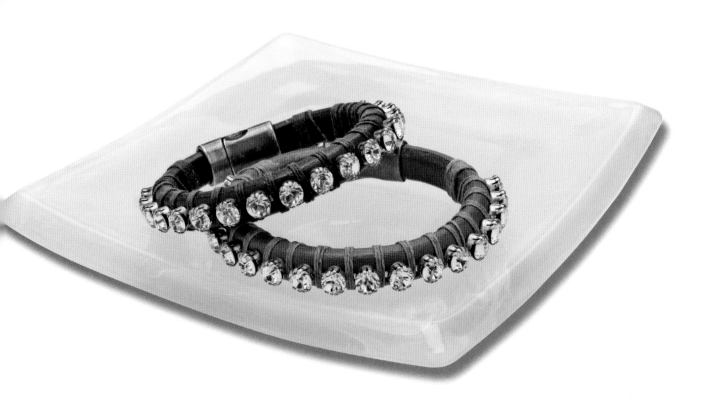

Leather & chain
bracelet & earrings

To show off cup chain, **Susan Sudnik** simply attaches it to leather with waxed linen thread. Go with a matching shade or add a contrasting color for visual pop. Play around with color combos and whip up a bunch!

1 **bracelet** • Cut a 6–7½-in. (15–19.1 cm) piece of cup chain (notes, p. 66). Center it on a leather cord. Apply glue to the end cup and press it to the leather. Allow to dry.

2 About ¼ in. (6 mm) from the glued cup chain, glue one end of waxed linen thread to the back of the leather. Make eight or nine wraps over the glued end and around the leather.

3 Between the first and second cup of the cup chain, wrap the waxed linen three times around the cup chain and the leather.

4 Continue wrapping the waxed linen three times between each cup until you've attached the entire cup chain, making sure to keep the leather curved as you work. Glue the end cup to the leather.

5 Make eight or nine wraps around the leather. Trim the waxed linen and glue the end to the leather and the wraps. Allow to dry.

6 Apply glue to one end of the leather and the inside of half of a magnetic clasp. Insert the leather into the clasp. Repeat on the other end. Allow to dry.

notes •••

- Order the leather in the length you need; the clasp adds about 1 in. (2.5 cm). If you must cut it, use a sharp kitchen knife and be careful not to distort the end; if you do, it won't fit into the clasp.
- Make sure the leather is curved before you measure how much cup chain to cut. Plan to leave about 1 in. (2.5 cm) of the leather unembellished at each end.

1 **earrings** • For each earring: Cut a cup from a piece of cup chain. Apply glue to the bezel of an earring wire. Place the cup in the bezel. Allow to dry.

2 On a headpin, string a teardrop bead. Make the first half of a wrapped loop **(Basics)**. Attach the loop of the earring wire and complete the wraps, overlapping the wire.

materials

bracelet

- 6½–8 in. (16.5–20 cm) Regaliz leather cord, 10 mm wide
- 6–7½ in. (15–19.1 cm) cup chain, 6 mm crystals
- 7–10 ft. (2.13–3.05 m) waxed linen thread, 3 ply
- magnetic clasp for Regaliz leather
- Loctite Super Glue Gel Control
- diagonal wire cutters

earrings

- 2 12–14 mm teardrop beads
- ½ in. (1.3 cm) cup chain, 6 mm crystals
- 2 2-in. (5 cm) headpins
- pair of lever-back earring wires with bezels
- chainnose and roundnose pliers
- Loctite Super Glue Gel Control

Stylish transfer
pendant

Making jewelry is never not about sharing. Everything you string shares a bit about you and your story. **Theresa Abelew's** pendant is inspired by two of her loves: resin and crossword puzzles. She transfers a completed crossword puzzle to a resin pendant for this project; however, you can use whatever newsprint reflects your personality.

1 resin pendant • Cover your work surface with waxed paper. Mix equal amounts part A and part B mold elements, working quickly. Roll the putty into a ball and flatten it slightly. Place the putty on the waxed paper and evenly press in a pendant, front side down. Wait about five minutes and remove the pendant.

2 Mix the resin according to the package instructions. Slowly pour the resin into the mold. Do not overfill. Allow to cure as directed.

3 Release the piece by gently flexing the mold. File the edges if necessary.

4 Use a paintbrush to apply a thin layer of resin to the front of the pendant (the side that was face down in the mold). Let dry.

5 On the back of the pendant, apply one or two coats of clear nail polish, allowing to dry between coats (see tips, below). Use a cotton ball with rubbing alcohol to gently remove any dirt and dust from handling.

6 Place the newsprint face down on the back of the pendant. Dab the newsprint with rubbing alcohol, applying direct, even pressure for several seconds (tips, p. 69). Remove the newsprint and let the alcohol dry.

7 If desired, apply a thin layer of colored nail polish to the back of the pendant. Apply additional coats as desired, letting each layer dry (see tips, below).

note •••

To make the mold, you can use any go-go or donut pendant you already have at home — otherwise, a Google search for "40 mm go-go pendant" brings up a lot of options.

tips •••

- Adding colored nail polish is optional, but without it the transferred print will be hard to see. When adding colored polish to the back of the pendant, stick to light, bright shades for the best results.
- It doesn't matter whether the nail polish is shimmery or opaque.
- To avoid chipping or scuffing the colored nail polish, seal the pendant with a thin layer or two of clear nail polish. Depending on the wear and tear on your piece, you may need to reapply a clear coat from time to time.
- If you've finished making the pendant and don't like your color choice or newsprint transfer, start over by using nail polish remover. It won't harm the resin, but be sure to wash the pendant with hot, soapy water and dry it completely before applying fresh nail polish and attempting a new transfer.

note ●●●

For this project, only apply nail polish on top of resin. If you add resin over nail polish, the resin will not cure.

1 **necklace** • Cut a 23–25 in. (58–64 cm) piece of rubber tubing, cord, or silk ribbon and two 3–4-in. (7.6–10 cm) pieces of 22- or 24-gauge wire. On each end, fold back the tubing to make a loop. Wrap a wire around the loop. Tuck the end of the wire.

2 Open the loop of a hook clasp **(Basics)**. Attach one end of the tubing and close the loop.

3 Attach the cord to the pendant with a lark's head knot **(Basics)**.

materials

resin pendant
- **40 mm go-go or donut pendant**
- Ice Resin
- MegaMold silicone RTV molding compound
- cotton balls
- nail polish, clear and colored
- newspaper
- paintbrush
- rubbing alcohol
- waxed paper
- metal file (optional)

necklace 18 in. (46 cm)
- resin pendant
- 23–25 in. (58-64 cm) rubber tubing, cord, or ribbon
- 6–8 in. (15-20 cm) 22- or 24-gauge wire
- hook clasp
- two pairs of pliers
- diagonal wire cutters

MegaMold silicone RTV molding compound from Cool Tools, cooltools.us.

tips ●●●

- Always transfer onto a smooth, even coat of dry nail polish — the newsprint will only transfer onto nail polish, never resin.
- If you are transferring text, be aware of the word fragments that will appear on the pendant.
- Don't rub the newspaper with the wet cotton ball as it can destroy the newspaper and ruin the transfer. Instead, dab it.
- You can carefully lift the newsprint to check the edge of the pendant and see how dark the transfer is, but be careful when setting the paper back down — if it's not aligned, you may end up with a "ghosting" of the print.

Stick to pearls
necklace & earrings

With these metal stick-pearl style connectors, **Irina Miech** envisions a long necklace made from natural pearls in all shapes and sizes (which add depth and texture). The stormy gray pearls have deep flashes of purple — it's these brilliant hues that unify the look.

components

pearl connectors • Cut a 3-in. (7.6 cm) piece of 22-gauge wire. Make a wrapped loop **(Basics)**. String a 6 mm round pearl and make a wrapped loop. Make 12 6 mm round-pearl connectors and six 10 mm rectangular-pearl connectors.

metal stick-pearl connector units • Open two jump rings **(Basics)**. Attach one to each hole of a metal stick-pearl connector and close the jump rings. Make three stick-pearl connector units.

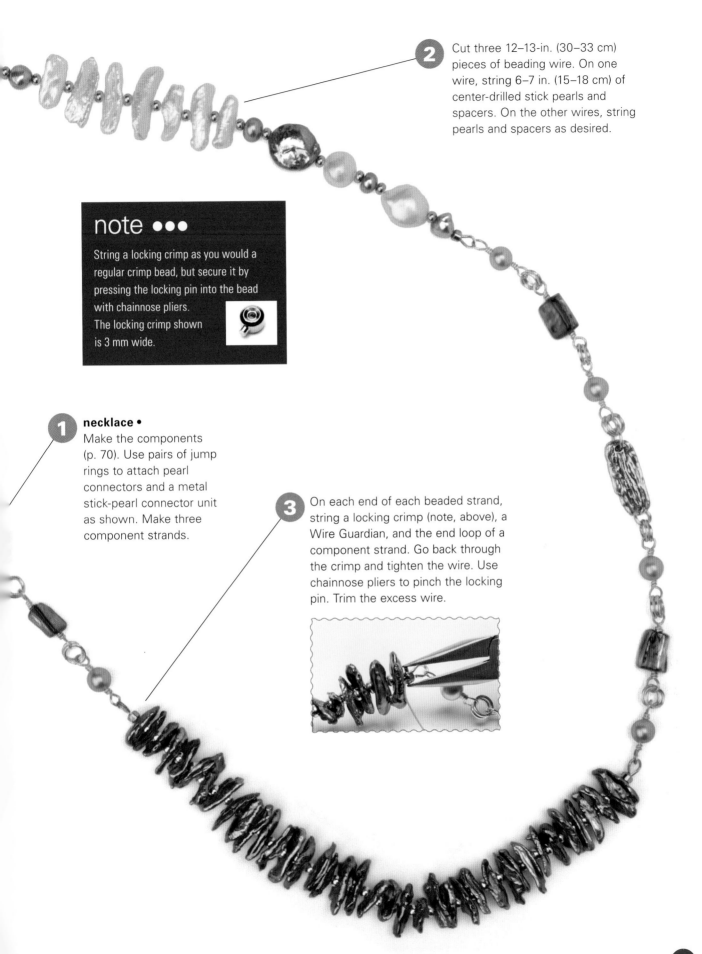

2 Cut three 12–13-in. (30–33 cm) pieces of beading wire. On one wire, string 6–7 in. (15–18 cm) of center-drilled stick pearls and spacers. On the other wires, string pearls and spacers as desired.

note •••

String a locking crimp as you would a regular crimp bead, but secure it by pressing the locking pin into the bead with chainnose pliers. The locking crimp shown is 3 mm wide.

1 **necklace •**
Make the components (p. 70). Use pairs of jump rings to attach pearl connectors and a metal stick-pearl connector unit as shown. Make three component strands.

3 On each end of each beaded strand, string a locking crimp (note, above), a Wire Guardian, and the end loop of a component strand. Go back through the crimp and tighten the wire. Use chainnose pliers to pinch the locking pin. Trim the excess wire.

Design alternative

Highlight center-drilled stick pearls in a shorter necklace.

materials

necklace 37 in. (94 cm)

- ◆ **7–10** 15–20 mm stick pearls, center drilled
- ◆ **40–50** 12–14 mm stick pearls, center drilled
- ◆ **3–6** 14–15 mm stick pearls
- ◆ **3–6** 11–12 mm coin pearls
- ◆ **6** 10 mm rectangular pearls
- ◆ **6–9** 8–10 mm round pearls
- ◆ **12** 6 mm round pearls
- ◆ **14–17** 4–6 mm assorted pearls
- ◆ **70–85** 2–3 mm spacers
- ◆ **3** 20 mm metal stick-pearl connectors
- ◆ flexible beading wire, .014 or .015
- ◆ 54 in. (1.4 m) 22-gauge wire
- ◆ **42** 6 mm jump rings
- ◆ **6** locking crimps
- ◆ **6** Wire Guardians
- ◆ chainnose and roundnose pliers
- ◆ diagonal wire cutters

earrings

- ◆ **2** 11–12 mm coin pearls
- ◆ **2** 20 mm metal stick-pearl connectors
- ◆ **2** 2-in. (5 cm) headpins
- ◆ **10** 6 mm jump rings
- ◆ pair of earring wires
- ◆ chainnose and roundnose pliers
- ◆ diagonal wire cutters

Supplies from Eclectica, eclectica beads.com.

1 **earrings** • For each earring: On a headpin, string a pearl. Make a wrapped loop **(Basics)**.

2 Open two jump rings **(Basics)**. Attach the loop of the pearl unit and close the jump rings.

3 Attach a pair of jump rings to the first pair.

4 Attach a single jump ring and a stick-pearl connector.

5 Attach the dangle and the loop of an earring wire.

Flirty flower
bangle

Bangles are so easy to wear, and **Jennifer Short** offers this equally simple way of decorating them. The ethereal colors work nicely together and can be worn with anything. She also likes the contrast of hard (bangle) and soft (ribbon) textures in these wrist corsages.

1 bracelet • Cut an 18-in. (46 cm) piece of wire. String five teardrop beads. Cross the wires, leaving a 6-in. (15 cm) tail on one end.

2 Wrap the working wire (the longer end) twice around two adjacent beads. (Don't pull too hard on the wire, or you'll risk breaking the beads.)

3 Continue wrapping the working wire around adjacent pairs of beads until you've wrapped all of the beads (tip, p. 74).

4

5

6

7

8

9

materials

bracelet

- **3** 10–12 mm glass leaf beads, top drilled
- **10** 8 mm glass teardrop beads, top drilled
- 3 ft. (.9 m) 24- or 26-gauge wire
- 18 in. (46 cm) ribbon, ¼–½ in. (6–13 mm) diameter
- bangle or cuff bracelet
- chainnose pliers
- diagonal wire cutters
- scissors

Make lots of stuff, of all kinds! The more you do, the better you become. It's all good practice, exercising both your technical and creative muscles.

4 On the working wire, string a leaf bead. Wrap each end two or three times around a bangle.

5 Use the tail wire to attach another leaf to the bangle. Trim the excess wire.

6 Make a second flower. Attach the flower and a leaf to the bangle so the flowers are asymmetrical.

7 Wrap the wires to secure the flowers to the bangle. Trim the excess wire. (This is the back view of the bangle.)

8 Cut an 18-in. (46 cm) piece of ribbon. Center the ribbon on the bangle, next to one of the flowers. Wrap each end around the bangle, between the leaves and flowers, covering the wire wraps.

9 Tie the ends in a bow and trim the excess.

tip ●●●

When you wrap the wire around pairs of beads, you'll likely end up with a neat appearance from the front. I prefer the back view; it's more fun and asymmetrical. The choice is yours.

Lush loops
necklace & earrings

Karen Harris loves the versatility and accessibility
of bead chips. And, unlike with the tasty potato
variety, she can indulge without feeling guilty.

loop segment • Cut a 5-in. (13 cm) piece of .010 or .012 beading wire. String a micro crimp bead, 2½ in. (6.4 cm) of color A chips interspersed with three or four color B chips, and a micro crimp. On each end, go back through a few beads just strung to make a loop (tip, right). Make a flattened crimp **(Basics)** and trim the excess wire. Make 25 loop segments.

tip ●●●

I used micro crimps for the loop segments in the turquoise version because I wanted them to be less prominent in the design.

• With micro crimps, finer (.010 or .012) beading wire is necessary. Irregular beads can create gaps in the wire. Before finishing the loop segments and the main strand, shift the beads to eliminate gaps.

• When crimping, use roundnose pliers to maintain the loop while tightening the wire.

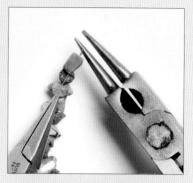

• If you prefer, feel free to use standard crimp beads and heavier beading wire throughout the entire design.

1 necklace • Cut a piece of .014 or .015 beading wire **(Basics)**. On the wire, center three color B chips, both loops of a loop segment, and three color Bs.

2 On each end, string both loops of a loop segment and three color Bs. Repeat until you've strung all of the loop segments. String color Bs until the strand is within 1 in. (2.5 cm) of the finished length.

3 Open a 7 mm jump ring **(Basics)** and attach a lobster claw clasp or 7mm split ring. Close the jump ring. On one end, string a crimp bead and the jump ring. Check the fit and add or remove beads if necessary. Go back through the beads just strung and tighten the wire. Crimp the crimp bead **(Basics)** and trim the excess wire. Repeat on the other end, substituting a 10 mm jump ring or split ring for the 7 mm jump ring and clasp.

materials

necklace 23 in. (58 cm)

- **2** 34-in. (86 cm) strands 4–8 mm (small) chips, color A
- 34-in. (86 cm) strand 4–8 mm (small) chips, color B
- flexible beading wire, .014 or .015
- flexible beading wire, .010 or .012
- 10 mm jump ring or split ring
- 7 mm jump ring or split ring
- **2** crimp beads
- **50** micro crimp beads
- lobster claw clasp
- chainnose and roundnose pliers

- diagonal wire cutters
- micro crimping pliers (optional)

earrings

- **2** 4–8 mm chips, color B
- **4** 4–8 mm chips, color A
- **2** 18 mm hammered oval links
- **2** 1½-in. (3.8 cm) decorative headpins
- **2** 5–6 mm jump rings
- pair of earring wires
- chainnose and roundnose pliers
- diagonal wire cutters

1

2

3

1 **earrings** • For each earring: On a decorative headpin, string a color A chip, a color B chip, and a color A. Make the first half of a wrapped loop **(Basics)**.

2 Attach an oval link and complete the wraps.

3 Use chainnose pliers to turn the loop of an earring wire so it's perpendicular to the wire. Open a jump ring **(Basics)** and attach the dangle and the earring wire's loop. Close the jump ring.

"
IT'S REALLY EASY TO GET COLORS RIGHT. IT'S REALLY HARD TO GET BLACK AND NEUTRALS RIGHT

-DONNA KARAN

"

Textured
three-strand
necklace & earrings

Creating a multistrand necklace with a wide deer hide base is simpler than it looks. **Marcy Kentz** pairs pearls with soft leather and adds bright vermeil accents like links, spacers, and dangles. The result is a contemporary take on a classic three-strand necklace.

1 **necklace** • Cut two 8-in. (20 cm) pieces of leather. Trim each end to a rounded, tapered shape.

2 Using a micro-hole punch, punch one hole ¾ in. (1.9 cm) from the center of the taper. Punch a hole equally spaced on each side in a straight line. Punch one hole on the other end. Repeat with the other piece of leather.

3 Cut three 12-in. (30 cm) pieces of beading wire. On the first wire, center 12 dangles alternating with 4 mm beads. On each end, string five to nine 4 mm beads. On the second

wire, center a 5 mm spacer. On each end, string three 5 mm beads alternating with three 4 mm spacers, then four to eight 5 mm beads. On the third wire, center five three-circle links alternating with four 6 mm beads. On each end, string eight to 12 6 mm beads.

4 On each end of each wire, string the corresponding hole of the leather and a crimp bead (tip, below). Go back through the crimp bead to form a loop with the wire. Make a flattened crimp **(Basics)**.

tip ●●●

To ensure the wire does not slip through the hole, string a spacer or seed bead before stringing the crimp bead in step 4.

5 Apply glue to the leather ends and spread it to the edges with your fingers. Fold the ends back and press them together. Allow to dry. Place a heavy object over the glued ends to help them dry flat.

6 Cut two 3-in. (7.6 cm) pieces of 22-gauge wire. On each end, make the first half of a large wrapped loop **(Basics)**. String the hole on one end and complete the wraps. String a 4 mm spacer and make the first half of a wrapped loop. Attach half of a toggle clasp and complete the wraps. Repeat on the other end.

Design alternative

Suspend a variety of pendants, dangles, spacers, and chain from knotted leather cord for mixed-metal appeal.

materials

necklace 20 in. (51 cm)
- 8-in. (20 cm) strand 6 mm beads
- 8-in. (20 cm) strand 5 mm beads
- 8-in. (20 cm) strand 4 mm beads
- **5** 20 mm three-circle links
- **3** 5 mm spacers
- **6** 4 mm spacers
- **6** 5 mm flat spacers (optional)
- **12** 1 mm dangles
- flexible beading wire, .014 or .015
- 16 in. (41 cm) leather, 20 mm wide
- 6 in. (13 cm) 22-gauge wire
- **6** crimp beads
- toggle clasp
- chainnose and roundnose pliers
- diagonal wire cutters
- micro-hole punch
- scissors
- The Ultimate craft glue

earrings
- 2 5 mm beads
- 2 4 mm spacers
- 2 37 mm three-circle links
- 2 1½-in. (3.8 cm) headpins
- 4 4 mm jump rings
- pair of earring wires
- chainnose and roundnose pliers
- diagonal wire cutters

1

2

1 **earrings •** For each earring: On a headpin, string a spacer and a bead. Make the first half of a wrapped loop **(Basics)**.

2 Attach the smallest link of a three-circle link and complete the wraps.

3

3 Open a jump ring **(Basics)**. Attach the center link and the loop of an earring wire. Close the jump ring. Attach a second jump ring.

Study in contrasts
necklace, bracelet, & earrings

This necklace is held together (figuratively speaking!) by the attraction of opposites: black and cream, matte and sparkle, vintage and modern. Although **Naomi Fujimoto** usually prefers odd numbers, in this project she opts for six strands — enough to make a statement, but not so many as to make finishing difficult.

necklace finishing

1 On each side, over all six wires, string a teardrop. Check the fit, allowing about 2 in. (5 cm) for the clasp, and add or remove beads if necessary (tip, p. 83).

2 On one side, over all six wires, string a round bead, a crimp tube, and a lobster claw clasp. Repeat on the other side, substituting a 2-in. (5 cm) chain for the clasp. Go back through the crimp tube and round bead and tighten the wires. Crimp the crimp tubes **(Basics)** and trim the excess wire.

3 Use chainnose pliers or a Mighty Crimper to close a crimp cover over each crimp.

4 On a headpin, string a teardrop. Make the first half of a wrapped loop **(Basics)**. Attach the end link and complete the wraps.

tip ●●●

If you want a bolder necklace, string more strands using .010 or .012 beading wire, or string a large-hole bead in step 1 of the finishing.

3 Arrange the strands so three of them point the opposite direction. Finish the necklace (p. 82).

1

necklace •
For the shortest strand: Cut a 19–21-in. (48–53 cm) piece of beading wire. String three to six rondelles and a teardrop bead. Repeat until the strand is within 6 in. (15 cm) of the finished length, ending with rondelles.

2 Cut five more pieces of beading wire, each 1½ in. (3.8 cm) longer than the previous piece. On each wire, repeat the pattern from step 1.

tip ●●●

Vary the number of rondelles to change the length of each strand.

1

bracelet • Cut a piece of beading wire **(Basics)**. String rondelles until the strand is within 1½ in. (3.8 cm) of the finished length.

Usually I go for colorful beads, but I couldn't resist the visual pop of black, cream, and pyrite.

On one end, string a 4 mm crystal, a crimp bead, a 4 mm, and a lobster claw clasp. Repeat on the other end, substituting a chain link for the clasp. Check the fit, and add or remove beads if necessary. Go back through the beads just strung and tighten the wire. Crimp the crimp bead **(Basics)** and trim the excess wire.

2

3

Attach a crimp cover over each crimp. On a headpin, string a 12 mm crystal. Make the first half of a wrapped loop **(Basics)**. Attach the end link and complete the wraps.

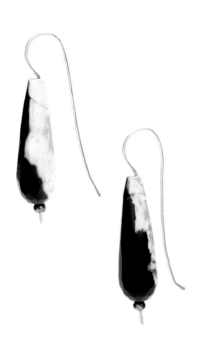

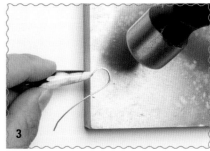

1 **earrings •** Set aside two rondelles that will accommodate 20-gauge wire. For each earring: Cut a 4-in. (10 cm) piece of wire. Hammer the end of the wire to form a paddle shape.

2 String a rondelle and a teardrop bead. Make a right-angle bend, then wrap the wire around a pen barrel. Trim the wire to about the length of the teardrop. File the end.

3 On a bench block, gently hammer each side of the wire.

tip ●●●

Consider teardrop beads that are not only uniformly shaped but have pleasing contrasts. The project uses beads with cream and beige visible from any angle.

Design alternative

Silver pyrite rondelles
make a glittery bib
for a special occasion.

tip •••

Before attaching the clasp or extender
chain, trim the beading wire so the ends
are flush. It will be easier to string all of
the wires together back through the crimp
tube and spacer.

notes •••

- The teardrop beads are dyed black-and-
  white agates; the rondelles are pyrite.
- The pyrite-colored crystals on the ends
  of the bracelet are Swarovski Elements
  crystal Dorado 2X.
- Try bronze beading wire; it's a great
  match with antiqued brass findings.

materials

necklace 18 in. (46 cm)
- **6** 15-in. (38 cm) strands 30 mm
  faceted teardrop beads
- **3** 13½-in. (34.3 cm) strands
  3 mm faceted rondelles
- **2** 9–11 mm large-hole
  round beads
- flexible beading wire, .014 or .015
- 2-in. headpin
- **2** 3 mm crimp tubes
- **2** 7 mm crimp covers
- lobster claw clasp
- 2 in. (5 cm) chain, 10–12 mm links
- chainnose pliers

- diagonal wire cutters
- Mighty Crimper (optional)

bracelet
- 12 mm round crystal
- **4** 4 mm round crystals
- **50–60** 3 mm faceted rondelles,
  left over from necklace
- chain link, 10–12 mm
- flexible beading wire, .014 or .015
- 2-in. (5 cm) headpin
- **2** crimp beads
- **2** crimp covers

- lobster claw clasp
- chainnose or crimping pliers
- diagonal wire cutters

earrings
- **2** 30 mm faceted teardrop beads
- **2** 3 mm faceted rondelles
- 8 in. (20 cm) 20-gauge wire
- diagonal wire cutters
- hammer and bench block
- metal file or emery board
- pen

Breakout buttons
bangles & earrings

Chances are you've seen beaded wire bangles, or maybe you've even wired beads to hoops. In these projects, **Becky Nunn** shows you how to take the wired bangle to the next level by adding rhinestone chain, some beads, and a crafty charm. Make a bunch and you can be wrist-deep in trendsetting style.

1 cup-chain bangle • a Cut a 9-in. (23 cm) piece of cup chain.

b Cut a 48-in. (1.2 m) piece of 24-gauge wire. Place the cup chain on a bangle. Leaving a 2-in. (5 cm) tail, make three wraps around the bangle between the first two cups.

2a Continue making three wraps between cups until you've attached all of the chain to the bangle. Trim chain if necessary.

b End by wrapping wire around the bangle between the beginning and end of the chain. Trim the wire and tuck the ends.

beaded cup-chain bangle • Cut 11 three-link pieces of cup chain. Follow step 1b of the cup-chain bangle. Make three wraps between the next two cups and again after the third cup. String a bead and make three wraps between the three-link pieces. Repeat step 2b of the cup-chain bangle.

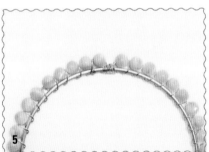

1 button-charm bangle • Measure equal parts of Crystal Clay. You'll need about a pea-size amount of combined clay. Use your fingers to mix the clay together for at least four minutes.

2 Fill a bezel with clay. The top should be level with the edge, not domed.

3 Place a button on the clay and press it down lightly, allowing some clay to push up through the holes of the button.

4 Use a toothpick topped with putty or wax to pick up a bead cap. Press it into the clay. Repeat with a rhinestone. Allow the clay to cure on a flat surface for 24 hours.

5 Cut a 48-in. (1.2 m) piece of 24-gauge wire. Leaving a 2-in. (5 cm) tail, make a wrap, string a bead, and make a wrap. Continue until you've covered the bangle with beads. End by wrapping wire around the bangle between the first and last beads. Trim the wire and tuck the ends.

6 Open a jump ring **(Basics)** and attach the charm to the bangle. Close the jump ring.

1 **button-charm earrings**
• Follow steps 1 to 4 of the button-charm bangle to make two button charms.

2 For each earring: Open the loop of an earring wire **(Basics)** and attach the charm. Close the loop.

1 **chaton earrings** •
Follow steps 1 and 2 of the button-charm bangle to make two bezels. For each bezel: Use a toothpick topped with putty or wax to pick up a 2 mm chaton. Press it into the clay near the edge of the bezel. Fill the outer edge of the bezel with 2 mm chatons. Press a 6 mm chaton into the center of the bezel. Allow the clay to cure for 24 hours.

2 For each earring: Cut a ½-in. (1.3 cm) piece of chain. On a headpin, string a bead and make a plain loop **(Basics)**. Open the loop **(Basics)** and attach an end link of chain. Close the loop. Attach a jump ring and the remaining end link.

materials

cup-chain bangle
- 9 in. (23 cm) cup chain
- 48 in. (1.2 m) 24-gauge wire
- 2¾ in. (7 cm) metal bangle
- chainnose or bentnose pliers
- diagonal wire cutters

beaded cup-chain bangle
- 11 5 mm beads
- 6½ in. (16.5 cm) cup chain
- 48 in. (1.2 m) 24-gauge wire
- 2¾ in. (7 cm) metal bangle
- chainnose or bentnose pliers
- diagonal wire cutters

button-charm bangle
- 42–45 5 mm beads
- 13 mm button
- 6 mm bead cap
- 20 mm round bezel charm

- cup with rhinestone, trimmed from cup chain
- 48 in. (1.2 m) 24-gauge wire
- 2¾ in. (7 cm) metal bangle
- Crystal Clay, dark brown
- 10 mm jump ring or chain link
- 2 pairs of pliers, including chainnose or bentnose pliers
- diagonal wire cutters
- toothpick
- wax or putty

button-charm earrings
- 2 13 mm buttons
- 2 6 mm bead caps
- 2 20 mm round bezel charms
- 2 cups with rhinestones, trimmed from cup chain
- Crystal Clay, dark brown
- pair of earring wires

- 2 pairs of pliers
- toothpick
- wax or putty

chaton earrings
- 2 5 mm beads
- 2 6 mm crystal chatons
- 20–22 2 mm crystal chatons
- 1 in. (2.5 cm) chain, 2 mm links
- 2 1-in. (2.5 cm) headpins
- 2 4 mm jump rings
- pair of 14 mm round bezel earrings
- Crystal Clay, dark brown
- pair of earring wires
- chainnose and roundnose pliers
- diagonal wire cutters
- toothpick
- wax or putty

Woven crystal and chain
necklace & earrings

Want a fun way to use just a few inches of chain? **Samantha Mitchell** weaves a strand of beads through the links. The simple pattern of crystals and pearls looks like it's floating inside the textured metal structure. Mixing in satin cord keeps the necklace shimmery, but casual enough to wear every day.

1

2

3

4

5

6

materials

necklace 17 in. (43 cm)

- **12–16** 6 mm bicone crystals
- **7–9** 3 mm bicone crystals
- **6–8** 6 mm round pearls
- flexible beading wire, .010
- 26–30 in. (66–76 cm) satin cord, 2 mm
- 5½–6½ in. (14–16.5 cm) double-link chain, 24–25 mm links
- **2** 6–7 mm soldered jump rings
- **2** 4–5 mm jump rings
- **2** crimp ends
- lobster claw clasp
- **2** pairs of pliers
- diagonal wire cutters
- crimping pliers (optional)

earrings

- **2** 6 mm bicone crystals
- **2** 3 mm bicone crystals
- **2** 5–6 mm round pearls
- **2** 1½-in. (3.8 cm) headpins
- pair of kidney-style earring wires
- chainnose and roundnose pliers
- diagonal wire cutters

1 necklace • a Cut a 5½–6½-in. (14–16.5 cm) piece of chain and two 13–15-in. (33–38 cm) pieces of cord.

b Make a lark's head knot **(Basics)** around a soldered jump ring and a pair of end links.

2 Cut a 12–13-in. (30–33 cm) piece of beading wire. String a crimp bead and a jump ring from step 1. Go back through the crimp bead and tighten the wire. Crimp the crimp bead **(Basics)**.

3 String a 3 mm bicone crystal, a 6 mm bicone crystal, a pearl, and a 6 mm bicone. Repeat five to seven times, ending with a 3 mm.

4 Weave the beaded strand through the chain links. String a crimp bead and the remaining jump ring. Go back through the last few beads strung and tighten the wire. Crimp the crimp bead and trim the excess wire.

5 Check the fit, and trim cord if necessary. On each pair of cord ends, string a crimp end. Using chainnose pliers, flatten the middle portion of the crimp end **(Basics)**.

6 Open a 4–5 mm jump ring **(Basics)**. Attach a lobster claw clasp and a crimp end. On the other end, attach a jump ring.

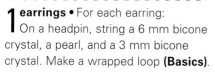

1

2

1 earrings • For each earring: On a headpin, string a 6 mm bicone crystal, a pearl, and a 3 mm bicone crystal. Make a wrapped loop **(Basics)**.

2 Attach the dangle and the loop of an earring wire. Use chainnose pliers to close the loop.

Pearl
essence
necklace & earrings

The plain loop is a basic in your jewelry repertoire. Here, **Susanne Young** uses it to make dangles, connectors, and clusters, with each piece contributing to a beautiful whole. If you like, include both silver and gunmetal wire (plus earring wires in gold) for a subtle nod to the mixed-metal look.

1 necklace • On a headpin, string a 6 mm pearl in color A. Make a plain loop **(Basics)**. Make 32 to 40 pearl units, half in color A and half in color B.

2 Cut a 1⅛-in. (2.9 cm) piece of wire. On one end, make a plain loop. String a 10 mm pearl in color C and make a plain loop. Make 32 to 40 connectors, half in color C and half in color D.

3 Open a loop of a color C connector **(Basics)**. Attach a color A pearl unit and close the loop. Make 16 to 20 dangles attaching color C with A (C/A dangle). Make 16 to 20 dangles attaching color D with B (D/B dangle).

4 Cut a 1¾-in. (4.4 cm) piece of wire. On one end, make a plain loop. String a 10 mm pearl in color B, a C/A dangle, a D/B dangle, and a 10 mm pearl in color A. Make a plain loop. Make 16 to 20 clusters.

5 Open a loop of a cluster and attach a loop of another cluster. Close the loop. Attach the remaining clusters.

6 On one end, use a jump ring to attach a lobster claw clasp. On the other end, attach a jump ring.

1

2

1 earrings • For each earring: Follow necklace step 1 to make a pearl unit. Follow necklace step 2 to make a connector.

2 Open a loop of the connector **(Basics)**. Attach the pearl unit and close the loop.

3

3 Attach the dangle and the loop of an earring wire.

materials

necklace 21½ in. (54.6 cm)
- **64–80** 10 mm round pearls, in four colors: A, B, C, D
- **32–40** 6 mm round pearls, in two colors: A, B
- **64–80** in. (1.7–2.1 m) 22-gauge wire
- **32–40** 1-in. (2.5 cm) headpins
- **2** 5 mm jump rings
- lobster claw clasp
- chainnose and roundnose pliers
- diagonal wire cutters

earrings
- **2** 10 mm round pearls
- **2** 6 mm round pearls
- **2¼** in. (5.7 cm) 22-gauge wire
- **2** 1-in. (2.5 cm) headpins
- pair of earring wires
- chainnose and roundnose pliers
- diagonal wire cutters

tip ●●●

Use eye pins instead of wire for the connectors and clusters.

Keshi pearl
necklace, bracelet, & earrings

These bold statement pieces use the biggest keshi pearls **Naomi Fujimoto** can find, along with a second strand that's a bit smaller. Simply string and twist! Large-hole crystal pearls accommodate two strands of .014 or .015 beading wire and make for a finish that's both pretty and painless.

1 necklace • Cut two 16–18-in. (41–46 cm) pieces of beading wire. On each wire, string 10–12 in. (25–30 cm) of keshi pearls. On one wire, string 30–35 mm pearls, and on the other string 20–25 mm pearls. Tape the ends and gently twist the strands together.

2 Remove the tape. On each side, over both ends, string round pearls until the strand is within 1½ in. (3.8 cm) of the finished length.

3 On one side, over both ends, string a crimp bead, a spacer, and a lobster claw clasp. Repeat on the other side, substituting a 2-in. (5 cm) chain for the clasp. Check the fit and add or remove beads if necessary. Go back through the last few beads strung and tighten the wires. Crimp the crimp beads **(Basics)** and trim the excess wire.

4 Close a crimp cover over each crimp. On a headpin, string a round pearl. Make the first half of a wrapped loop **(Basics)**. Attach the end link of chain and complete the wraps.

1 bracelet • Cut two 13–14-in. (33–36 cm) pieces of beading wire. On each wire, string 3½–4 in. (8.9–10 cm) of keshi pearls. Tape the ends and gently twist the strands together.

2 Remove the tape. On each side, over both ends, string round pearls until the strand is within 1 in. (2.5 cm) of the finished length.

3 Follow step 3 of the necklace, substituting a 1-in. (2.5 cm) piece of chain for the 2-in. (5 cm) piece. Follow step 4 of the necklace.

materials

necklace 16½ in. (41.9 cm)

- ◆ 16-in. (41 cm) strand 30–35 mm keshi pearls
- ◆ 16-in. (41 cm) strand 20–25 mm keshi pearls
- ◆ **11–17** 12 mm large-hole round crystal pearls
- ◆ **2** 5–7 mm large-hole spacers
- ◆ flexible beading wire, .014 or .015
- ◆ 1½-in. (3.8 cm) headpin
- ◆ **2** crimp beads
- ◆ **2** crimp covers
- ◆ lobster claw clasp
- ◆ 2 in. (5 cm) chain for extender, 10–16 mm links
- ◆ chainnose and roundnose pliers
- ◆ diagonal wire cutters
- ◆ crimping pliers

bracelet

- ◆ **7–11** 30–35 mm keshi pearls, left over from necklace
- ◆ **8–12** 20–25 mm keshi pearls, left over from necklace
- ◆ **7–11** 12 mm large-hole round crystal pearls
- ◆ **2** 5–7 mm large-hole spacers
- ◆ flexible beading wire, .014 or .015
- ◆ 3½ in. (8.9 cm) 24-gauge wire
- ◆ 1½-in. (3.8 cm) headpin
- ◆ **2** crimp beads
- ◆ **2** crimp covers
- ◆ lobster claw clasp
- ◆ 1 in. (2.5 cm) chain for extender, 10–16 mm links
- ◆ chainnose and roundnose pliers
- ◆ diagonal wire cutters
- ◆ crimping pliers (optional)

earrings

- ◆ **2** 20–25 mm keshi pearls
- ◆ **2** chain links, 10–16 mm
- ◆ 7 in. (18 cm) 24-gauge wire
- ◆ pair of earring wires
- ◆ chainnose and roundnose pliers
- ◆ diagonal wire cutters

Keshi pearls from JP Pearl & Jewelry, Inc., jpjewelry@aol.com.

1

2

3

notes ●●●

- Choose round crystal pearls in vintage gold for their matte finish and to bring out the luminescence in the olive keshi pearls. If you prefer a glossier finish, try crystal pearls in bright gold; string antique brass pearls for a closer color match.
- The round-pearl bracelet uses bicone crystals in crystal Dorado 2X.

1 earrings • For each earring:
Cut a 3½-in. (8.9 cm) piece of wire. String a pearl and make a set of wraps above it **(Basics)**. Make the first half of a wrapped loop **(Basics)** perpendicular to the pearl.

2 Attach the loop and a chain link. Complete the wraps.

3 Open the loop of an earring wire **(Basics)**. Attach the dangle and close the loop.

Sail away
bracelet

Back in the day, a sailor would make bracelets from the extra ropes on his ship and give them to loved ones to wear for good luck at sea. Use **Jane Konkel's** modern update as a token of friendship, good luck, or just to proclaim your love for the water.

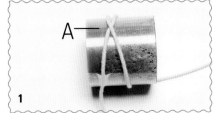

1 **bracelet •** Cut a 9-ft. (2.7 m) piece of macramé cord. Apply glue to the working end to stiffen it. Tape the other end to the left side of a cylindrical object. Make one wrap, crossing the cords to make an X (point A).

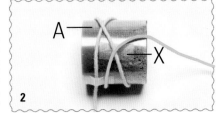

2 Make another wrap, bringing the working cord between the two fixed cords and crossing over the right cord to form another X (tip, p. 98). Tape the X.

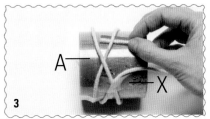

3 Above point A, string the working cord under the cord on the right.

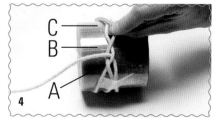

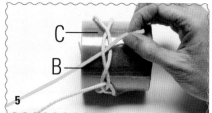

tip •••

Allow some slack when taping in step 2. You will need to double the plait and then triple it.

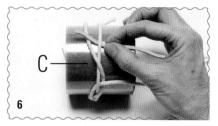

materials

bracelet

- 9 ft. (2.7 m) 2–3 mm macramé cord
- bracelet mandrel or other cylindrical object, 2¾ in. (7 cm) or 3 in. (7.6 cm) diameter
- Super New Glue
- scissors
- lighter (optional)

notes •••

- The version of this bracelet in the how-tos uses a candle with a 3-in. (7.6 cm) diameter. For smaller wrists, use a candle with a 2¾-in. (7 cm) diameter.
- This plait is from Suzen Millodot's book. You can find instructions for other knots in *Celtic Knots for Beaded Jewellery* by Suzen Millodot.
- Tie a water-themed charm to your rope bracelet with bright thread as a final finishing touch.

4 Cross the left fixed cord over the right. Note the new crossings at points B and C.

5 Between B and C, string the working cord under the left cord and over the right cord.

6 Above C, string the working cord under the right cord.

7 Cross the left fixed cord over the right as in step 4.

8 String the working cord under the left cord and over the right cord as in step 5.

9 Above the X, string the working cord under the right cord and then over the left cord as in step 6. Repeat steps 4, 5, and 6 until you reach the starting point. Remove the tape from step 2.

10 String the working cord following the path in steps 1 to 9 to double the plait. Continue until you reach the starting point.

11 Remove the bracelet from the cylinder. String the working cord through again, following the path to triple the plait.

12 String the ends to the inside of the bracelet. Trim the ends to ½ in. (1.3 cm).

13 If desired, use a lighter to seal the ends. Glue each end to the inside of the bracelet.

"
SILVER, GOLD

I DON'T DISCRIMINATE
-CHARLAINE HARRIS

"

Super hoop
earrings

While on vacation, **Ann Westby** tries to create jewelry with a minimum of supplies. These earrings need only 20-gauge wire. Once you learn this simple technique, you'll be able to make hoops in many different sizes — without a huge array of tools and materials.

1

2

3

4

5

6

materials

hoop earrings

- 30–36 in. (76–91 cm) 20-gauge half-hard wire
- chainnose and roundnose pliers
- diagonal wire cutters
- hammer and bench block
- metal file or emery board
- round mandrel or metal pipe
- pill bottle (optional)

tip ●●●

The first hammering (on the bench block) will give you a straight section of wire to work with. The second hammering (around the mandrel) will flatten any wire that popped up when you formed the hoop.

1 hoop earrings • For each earring: Cut a 15–18-in. (38–46 cm) piece of wire. Fold it in half over the jaw of the roundnose pliers and cross the ends below the jaw.

2 Cross each end around roundnose pliers again. Repeat until you've made a 5–7-in. (13–18 cm) section. Use chainnose pliers to straighten the section if it gets twisted as you go.

3 Wrap one wire around the other. Trim the excess wrapping wire and use chainnose pliers to tuck the end. Trim the remaining wire, leaving a ¾-in. (1.9 cm) tail.

4 On a bench block, hammer the crossed section. If desired, hammer the wire tail. File the end.

5 Wrap the wire around a pill bottle or mandrel to form a hoop. Use chainnose pliers to bend the tip of the tail upward.

6 Place the hoop on a mandrel or pipe. Hammer the crossed section of the wire, particularly at the joints where the wires cross. To close, latch the end through the first loop.

Design alternatives

Drape tiny rolo chain across a hoop and anchor it with wire.

Use 28-gauge wire to wrap gold-filled bead chain (Rio Grande, riogrande.com) to large hoops.

Marrakesh
multistrand
necklace & earrings

Leslie Rogalski's lush necklace layers three chains dripping with dangles for an alluring effect. Connectors hang from two of the chains, and the third features eye pins encased in rubber tubing and bicone crystals. The finished piece is a modern take on Moroccan silver jewelry.

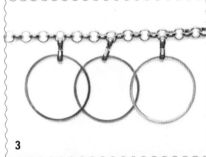

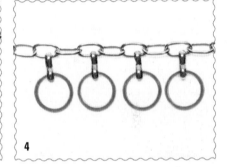

1 necklace • Open the loop of a connector **(Basics)**. Attach a quick link and use chainnose pliers to close the loop **(Basics)**. Make 19 20 mm units and 30 12 mm units.

2 Cut a ¾-in. (1.9 cm) piece of rubber tubing. On an eye pin, string a bicone crystal, the tubing, and a bicone. Make the first half of a wrapped loop **(Basics)**. Make 21 tube units.

3 Cut a 15–18-in. (38–46 cm) piece of rolo chain. Attach the center link and a 20 mm unit. On each end, skip five links and attach a 20 mm unit.

Attach the remaining 20 mm units on each side, skipping five links between each.

4 Cut a 16–19-in. (41–48 cm) piece of 7 mm cable chain. Attach a 12 mm unit to each of the links adjacent to the center link. On each side, skip a link and attach a 12 mm unit. Attach the remaining 12 mm units on each side, skipping a link between each.

5 Cut a 19–21-in. (48–53 cm) piece of 4 mm cable chain. Attach the center link and the loop of a tube unit. Complete the wraps. On each side,

skip seven links and attach a tube unit. Repeat until you've attached all of the bead units.

6 Open a 4 mm jump ring **(Basics)**. Attach an end link of 4 mm cable chain and close the jump ring. Repeat on the other end.

7 Use a 6 mm jump ring to attach the ends of each strand. On one end, use a connector to attach a spring-ring or lobster claw clasp. Repeat on the other end, substituting a 6 mm jump ring for the clasp.

materials

necklace 19 in. (48 cm)

- **42** 4 mm bicone crystals
- 16 in. (41 cm) rubber tubing
- 16–19 in. (41–48 cm) cable chain, 7 mm links
- 19–21 in. (48–53 cm) cable chain, 4 mm links
- 15–18 in. (38–46 cm) rolo chain, 4 mm links
- **49** Quick Links Connectors
- **19** 20 mm Quick Links
- **30** 12 mm Quick Links
- **21** 2-in. (5 cm) eye pins
- **3** 6 mm jump rings
- **2** 4 mm jump rings
- spring-ring or lobster claw clasp
- chainnose and roundnose pliers
- diagonal wire cutters

earrings

- **12** 4 mm bicone crystals
- 5 in. (13 cm) rubber tubing
- **2** 12 mm Quick Links
- **6** 2-in. (5 cm) eye pins
- pair of earring wires
- chainnose and roundnose pliers
- diagonal wire cutters

Quick Links and Quick Links Connectors from Beadalon, beadalon.com.

1 earrings • For each earring: Make three tube units as in step 2 of the necklace. Attach the tube units and a 12 mm Quick Link. Complete the wraps **(Basics)**.

2 Open the loop of an earring wire **(Basics)**. Attach the dangle and close the loop.

Design alternatives

Use the same techniques as in the necklace to connect chains and dangles in a three-strand gunmetal bracelet (right). Connect 12 mm Quick Links for cool, custom chain earrings (above right).

Poison pen
earrings

Sondra Barrington's steampunk-themed earrings use pen nibs with intriguing dabs of ink on the tips.

1

2

3

4

materials

earrings

- ◆ **8** 38 mm pen nibs
- ◆ **2** 8 mm crystal rondelles
- ◆ **2** 4 mm bicone crystals
- ◆ **2** 3 mm spacers
- ◆ **2** 2-in. (5 cm) eye pins
- ◆ **26** 4 mm jump rings
- ◆ pair of kidney-style earring wires
- ◆ chainnose and roundnose pliers
- ◆ diagonal wire cutters
- ◆ metal hole punch
- ◆ alcohol ink
- ◆ image transfer solution
- ◆ disposable mixing cup

Supplies from Rings & Things, rings-things.com.

1 earrings • Use a hole punch to punch a hole at the center of the top of each pen nib.

2 Mix ten drops of image transfer solution with five drops of alcohol ink. Dip each tip into the solution. Allow to dry completely.

3 For each earring: Open a jump ring **(Basics)**. Attach a nib. Close the jump ring. Attach four jump rings above and three jump rings below the jump ring with the attached nib. Use a jump ring to attach a nib and the bottom ring.

4 Use two jump rings to attach a nib to the second ring from the top. Use two jump rings to attach a nib to the third ring from the bottom.

5

6

5 On an eye pin, string a rondelle and make a plain loop **(Basics)**. On an earring wire, string a bicone crystal and a spacer.

6 Open a loop of the bead unit and attach the dangle. Attach the loop of the earring wire and the remaining loop of the bead unit.

tips ●●●

- Instead of a pliers-style hole punch, use a metal hole punch that won't flatten the nibs. A screw-down punch works well.
- You can allow the ink to dry overnight, or follow the image transfer solution directions to bake the painted nibs in a toaster oven.

I wanted to profile the pen nibs while adding a bit of sparkle and jingle.

Design alternative

Use three-to-one connectors dabbed with ink to showcase individual nibs.

Design on a dime
bracelet & earrings

Arlet Flores Soldevilla easily transforms budget-friendly materials — aluminum beads, brass spacers, and base metal chain — into a cuff that's greater than the sum of its parts. Even though crystals add to the cost, they accent the round beads with a pop of color. It's easy to change the style; just use round beads that are slightly larger than the chain links.

1 **bracelet • a** Cut two 6½–8-in. (16.5–20 cm) pieces of chain. Cut a 2-in. (5 cm) piece of wire. On one end, make a plain loop **(Basics)**. Make 20 to 28 eye pins.

b On an eye pin, string: spacer, third link of a chain, bicone crystal, color A round bead, bicone, third link of the other chain, spacer. Make a plain loop (tip, right).

tip ●●●

Because spacers have large holes, the bead units might seem a bit loose. Don't overtighten the loops, though, or the chain will be too stiff to curve around your wrist.

materials

bracelet

- 20–28 5–8 mm round beads, in four colors
- 40–56 4 mm bicone crystals
- 40–56 6 mm spacers
- 13–16 in. (33–41 cm) rolo chain, 4.5–5.5 mm links
- 40–56 in. (1–1.4 m) 20- or 22-gauge wire
- 4 5–6 mm jump rings
- two-strand slide clasp
- chainnose and roundnose pliers
- diagonal wire cutters

earrings

- 2 5–8 mm round beads
- 4 4 mm bicone crystals
- pair of earring threads
- chainnose and roundnose pliers
- diagonal wire cutters

2 Skipping a link, repeat step 1b with a color B round bead. Skipping a link, repeat with a color C round bead. Skipping a link, repeat with a color D round bead. String bead units through every other link, repeating the ABCD pattern, until the bracelet is within 1 in. (2.5 cm) of the finished length.

3 Trim chain if necessary, leaving the last two links open. Open a jump ring **(Basics)**. Attach an end link and the corresponding loop of half of a slide clasp. Close the jump ring. Use a jump ring to attach each remaining end link and the clasp.

1 **earrings •** For each earring: On a headpin, string a bicone crystal, a round bead, and a bicone. Make the first half of a wrapped loop **(Basics)**.

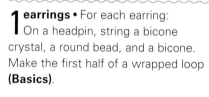

2 Attach the dangle and the loop of an earring thread. Complete the wraps.

Design alternative

Try gemstones or crystal pearls in place of the round aluminum beads. Also, change your choice of rolo chain and spacers to achieve a more vintage (or modern) look.

Bridal wave

necklace & cuff

Wedding season always is on the horizon, and **Kelsey Lawler** has brides on the brain. Inspired by her friend's unique style, this necklace befits a modern bride. A memory wire cuff partners well with the glamorous metal.

1

2

3

4

5

6

7

8

When designing wedding jewelry, always keep the bride's neckline, color scheme, venue, and overall style in mind.

1 **filigree necklace** • Cut a 3½-in. (8.9 cm) piece of wire. String a briolette and make a set of wraps above it **(Basics)**. Make the first half of a wrapped loop **(Basics)** perpendicular to the bead. Make seven briolette units.

2 Attach the loop of a briolette unit and the loop of a teardrop filigree and complete the wraps. Make six filigree units. Make one reverse filigree unit, attaching the briolette unit to the opposite end of the filigree.

3 Open a jump ring **(Basics)** and attach a filigree and a filigree unit

as shown. Close the jump ring. Make four two-filigree dangles.

4 Use two jump rings to attach two filigrees and a filigree unit as shown. Make a second three-filigree dangle the mirror image of the first.

5 Use three jump rings to attach three filigrees and the reverse filigree unit as shown. This is the center filigree dangle.

6 Cut a 16-in. (41 cm) piece of chain. Use a jump ring to attach the center link of chain and the center filigree dangle.

7 On each side, skip five links and use a jump ring to attach a two-filigree dangle. Attach a three-filigree dangle and the remaining two-filigree dangle, skipping five links between each.

8 Cut a 3-in. (7.6 cm) piece of wire. On one end, make the first half of a wrapped loop. String a round crystal and make the first half of a wrapped loop. Attach one loop and an end link of chain. Attach the other loop and half of a box clasp. Repeat on the other end.

materials

necklace 16 in. (41 cm)

- **18** 26 mm filigree teardrops
- **7** 11 mm crystal briolettes
- **2** 6 mm round crystals
- 31 in. (79 cm) 22-gauge wire
- 16 in. (41 cm) chain, 4 mm links
- **18** 5 mm jump rings
- box clasp
- chainnose and roundnose pliers
- diagonal wire cutters

cuff

- **85–125** 6 mm round pearls
- **12–15** 6 mm round crystals
- **8–12** 6 mm round beads
- **8–12** 6 mm spacers
- **5** 6 mm alphabet beads (optional)
- memory wire, bracelet diameter
- roundnose pliers
- heavy-duty wire cutters

Filigree teardrops from Fire Mountain Gems and Beads, firemountaingems.com. Filigree tube beads from faerynicethings.com.

note ●●●

The crystal briolettes are crystal golden shadow.

tip ●●●

If you're adding alphabet beads to your bracelet, make sure they stay front and center. Check the bead placement and alignment often, and remember that things will shift a bit when worn.

1 pearl cuff • Use heavy-duty wire cutters to cut a piece of memory wire with the desired number of coils. Use roundnose pliers to make a loop on one end.

2 String beads (tip, below) until the bracelet is within ¼ in. (6 mm) of the desired length. Make a loop.

Design alternative
Small monogrammed beads add a special touch to a bridal bracelet.

Grow fabulous flowers
necklace & bracelet

Brenda Schweder's *Now That's a Jig!* is a tool for making geometric shapes and repeatable components. As with any tool in the hands of an artist, the jig becomes an extension of that maker's vision, so her organic vision burst right through. The flower form is a go-to shape; it's as natural as nature itself.

flowers

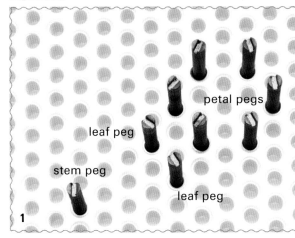

1 — petal pegs, leaf peg, stem peg, leaf peg

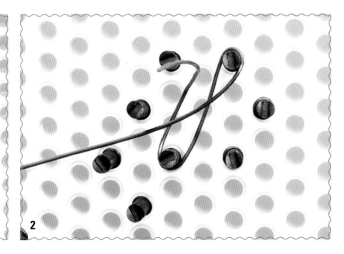

2

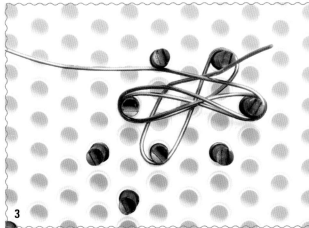

3

4

5

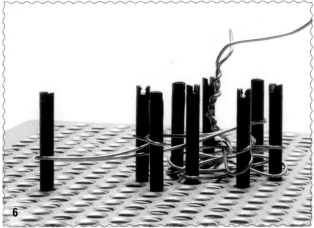

6

1 Set up nine pegs in a jig as shown.

2 Cut a 26-in. (66 cm) piece of wire. Make a right-angle bend 1½ in. (3.8 cm) from one end. With the tail pointing upward, wrap the working wire around two petal pegs in opposite directions to make a figure 8.

3 Make two figure 8s around an adjacent petal peg and the peg across from it.

4 Make two figure 8s around the last pair of petal pegs, bringing the wire toward the stem peg.

5 Wrap the wire around the stem peg. Make a figure 8 around the two leaf pegs.

6 Twist the working wire and tail together. Trim the excess wire. Use chainnose pliers or your fingers to push the petals of the flower together. Remove the flower from the jig.

materials

necklace 17 in. (43 cm)
- 78 in. (1.99 m) 20-gauge wire
- 11–14 in. (28–36 cm) chain, 3–4 mm links
- **4** 5–6 mm jump rings
- lobster claw clasp
- Now That's a Jig!
- chainnose pliers
- diagonal wire cutters

bracelet
- 26 in. (66 cm) 20-gauge square wire
- 8–10 in. (20–25 cm) chain, 2–3 mm links
- **3** 5 mm jump rings
- lobster claw clasp
- Now That's a Jig!
- chainnose pliers
- diagonal wire cutters

Supplies from Brenda Schweder, brendaschweder.etsy.com.

Go with the flow; the wire will go where it wants to — especially since it is one continuous piece.

1

3

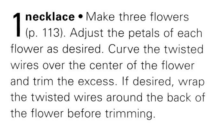

4

2

4

5

1 necklace • Make three flowers (p. 113). Adjust the petals of each flower as desired. Curve the twisted wires over the center of the flower and trim the excess. If desired, wrap the twisted wires around the back of the flower before trimming.

2 String a flower through the stem loop of a second flower. Use chainnose pliers to twist the intersections of the stem loop and petals.

3 Bend the stem loop of the first flower upward. String a third flower through the stem loop of the second flower. Bend the stem loop of the second flower upward.

4 Cut two 5½–7-in. (14–18 cm) pieces of chain. Open a jump ring **(Basics)**. Attach one or two petals of a flower and an end link of a chain. Close the jump ring. Attach the stem loop and an end link of the other chain.

5 On one end, use a jump ring to attach an end link and a lobster claw clasp. Repeat on the other end, omitting the clasp.

1

2

1 bracelet • Make a flower (p. 113). Cut two 4–5-in. (10–13 cm) pieces of chain. Open two jump rings **(Basics)**. Attach an end link and a petal of the flower. Close the jump rings.

2 Check the fit and trim chain if necessary. Use a jump ring to attach the pair of end links and a lobster claw clasp.

Turning over new leaves
necklace & earrings

Carol Ann Reim is always dreaming up ways to update old designs. For this one, three strands bring the filigree leaves to the center of the neckline to form a cascade. It drapes beautifully for a supple necklace.

components

1 **flower dangle** • Cut three ½–¾-in. (1.3–1.9 cm) pieces of 2 mm link chain. Open a 4 mm jump ring **(Basics)** and attach a 6º seed bead and an end link. Close the jump ring. Use a jump ring to attach another 6º. Attach three or four 6ºs to the other chains.

2 Cut a 2-in. (5 cm) piece of 21-gauge wire. Make a plain loop **(Basics)** on one end. Open the loop and attach the end link of each chain from step 1. Close the loop. String a 6º and a flower bead and make a plain loop. Make two flower dangles.

tube unit • On a headpin, string: bead cap, end cap tube charm, six to eight 6º seed beads, tube, end cap. Make a plain loop.

wire leaf • Cut a 5-in. (13 cm) piece of wire. Make a plain loop on one end. Using your fingers and roundnose pliers, curve the wire into a leaf shape about ¾ in. (1.9 cm) long. Wrap the end around the stem and down the middle of the leaf. Hammer each side of the leaf.

leaf unit • Cut a 2-in. (5 cm) piece of wire. Center a leaf bead and make a set of wraps above it **(Basics)**. Make a plain loop above the wraps.

coil unit • Cut a 1-in. (2.5 cm) piece of wire. Make a coil on one end. String a spacer and make a plain loop. Make six coil units.

necklace

1 **necklace** • Make the components (above). Cut a 2-in. (5 cm) piece of 3–5 mm link chain. Use pairs of 4 mm jump rings to attach the tube unit to one end and a flower dangle to the other. Cut a 3-in. (7.6 cm) piece of wire. Make the first half of a wrapped loop **(Basics)** and attach:

flower dangle, middle chain link, wire leaf, leaf unit. Complete the wraps. Make a wrapped loop.

2 Use a 5 mm jump ring to attach the wrapped loop and a filigree leaf. Use pairs of 4 mm jump rings to attach five filigree leaves. Use a

5 mm jump ring to attach the coil units to a pair of attached jump rings.

3 Cut three 8½-in. (21.6 cm) pieces of 3–5 mm link chain. Use pairs of jump rings to attach an end link to a filigree leaf.

4 Use pairs of jump rings to attach each end link to a marquise link. Use pairs of jump rings to attach a marquise link and the loop half of a toggle clasp.

5 Cut a 3–5-in. (7.6–13 cm) piece of 3–5 mm link chain. Use a pair of jump rings to attach a filigree leaf and an end link. Use pairs of jump rings to attach the remaining end link, two marquise links, and the bar half of the clasp.

1 earrings • For each earring: Make six coil units (p. 116). Open a 5 mm jump ring **(Basics)** and attach three units. Close the jump ring. Make two coil units.

2 Use a pair of 4 mm jump rings to attach the coil units and a marquise link.

3 Use a pair of 4 mm jump rings to attach another marquise link. Open the loop of a lever-back earring wire and attach the dangle. Close the loop.

materials

necklace 17 in. (43 cm)

- **5** 40 mm filigree leaves
- **3** 6 mm tube charm
- **2** 10 mm flower beads
- 15 mm leaf bead, top drilled
- **20–30** 6º seed beads, in two colors
- **6** 4 mm spacers
- 8 mm flower bead cap
- 20 in. (51 cm) 21-gauge wire
- 31–33 in. (79–84 cm) chain, 3–5 mm links
- 5 in. (13 cm) chain, 2 mm links
- **4** 10 mm marquise-shaped links
- **2** 5 mm jump rings
- **48** 4 mm jump rings
- 2½-in. (6.4 cm) headpin
- toggle clasp
- chainnose and roundnose pliers
- diagonal wire cutters
- hammer and bench block

earrings

- **4** 10 mm marquise-shaped links
- **12** 4 mm spacers
- **12** in. (30 cm) 21-gauge wire
- **4** 5 mm jump rings
- **8** 4 mm jump rings
- pair of earring wires
- chainnose and roundnose pliers
- diagonal wire cutters

"I LIKE LIGHT, COLOR, LUMINOSITY. I LIKE THINGS FULL OF COLOR AND VIBRANT

-OSCAR DE LA RENTA

Taffy garden
necklace & earrings

Catherine Hodge's necklace has a pastel palette with components in saltwater taffy shades like mint, coral, and ivory. In an effort to keep the style from becoming too romantic, steer away from filigree and dainty accents and instead choose chunkier metal findings.

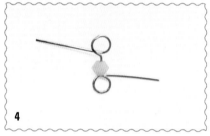

Be aware of trends and let them provide inspiration, but don't let them determine what you do and don't create.

1 necklace • Opposite the hole in each bottle cap bezel, punch a second hole. Glue a flower cabochon to each bezel. Allow to dry.

2 Cut a 3½-in. (8.9 cm) piece of wire. Make the first half of a wrapped loop **(Basics)**. String a bicone crystal, an 18 mm flower bead, and a bicone. Make the first half of a wrapped loop. Make four 18 mm flower units and two to six 14 mm flower units.

3 Cut a 3-in. (7.6 cm) piece of wire. Make the first half of a wrapped loop. String: bicone, spacer, helix crystal, spacer, bicone. Make the first half of a wrapped loop.

4 Cut a 2½-in. (6.4 cm) piece of wire. Make the first half of a wrapped loop. String a bicone and make the first half of a wrapped loop. Make four bicone connectors.

5 Attach a loop of a bicone connector and a hole of the 25 mm bezel. Complete the wraps. Repeat on the other side of the bezel.

6 On each side, attach an 18 mm bezel, bicone connector, and an 18 mm bezel. Complete the wraps as you go.

7 On each side, attach an 18 mm flower unit, an 18 mm link, an 18 mm flower unit, and a 10 mm link. Complete the wraps as you go.

Continue attaching 14 mm flower units and 10 mm links until the strand is within 2 in. (5 cm) of the finished length, ending with a link.

8 On one end, attach the link and a loop of the helix-crystal connector. Attach the remaining loop and a lobster claw clasp. Complete the wraps.

note ●●●

The bezel dimensions refer to the inside diameter of the bottle caps.

materials

necklace 20 in. (51 cm)
- 25 mm flower cabochon
- **4** 18 mm flower cabochons
- **4** 18 mm carved flower beads
- **2–6** 14 mm carved flower beads
- 8 mm helix crystal
- **18–26** 3 mm bicone crystals
- **2** 5 mm flat spacers
- 25 mm bottle cap bezel
- **4** 18 mm bottle cap bezels
- **2** 18 mm links
- **4–8** 10 mm links
- 34–48 in. (.86–1.22 m) 24-gauge wire
- lobster claw clasp
- chainnose and roundnose pliers

- diagonal wire cutters
- metal hole punch
- adhesive such as The Ultimate craft glue

earrings
- **2** 18 mm carved flower beads
- **6** 3 mm bicone crystals
- **4** 3 mm spacers
- **2** 10 mm links
- **2** 2½-in. (6.4 cm) decorative headpins
- pair of earring wires
- chainnose and roundnose pliers
- diagonal wire cutters

25 mm cabochon from Snapcrafty, snapcrafty.etsy.com; 18 mm cabochons from MK Supplies, mksupplies.etsy.com. Carved flower beads from McKenzie River Beads, mckenzieriverbeads.etsy.com, and Yummy Treasures, yummytreasures.etsy.com. Bottle cap bezels from Hobby Lobby, shophobbylobby.com. Links from Fire Mountain Gems and Beads, firemountaingems.com.

1 earrings • For each earring:
On a decorative headpin, string: flower bead, bicone crystal, spacer, bicone, spacer, bicone. Make the first half of a wrapped loop **(Basics)**.

2 Attach a link and complete the wraps. Open the loop of an earring wire **(Basics)** and attach the dangle. Close the loop.

Design alternative

To make one-of-a-kind pendants, glue cabochons on gunmetal charms (Arte Metal charms from Vintaj, vintaj.com).

Crescents of color
necklace & earrings

For **Jane Konkel,** these gorgeous enameled components are eye-catching, and they make her smile. Designing with these versatile crescents will have you smiling too, because you only need to know one technique — and every color combination looks radiant.

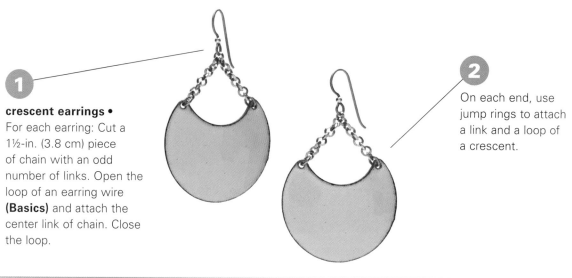

1

crescent earrings • For each earring: Cut a 1½-in. (3.8 cm) piece of chain with an odd number of links. Open the loop of an earring wire **(Basics)** and attach the center link of chain. Close the loop.

2

On each end, use jump rings to attach a link and a loop of a crescent.

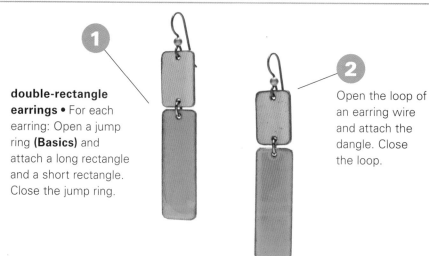

1

double-rectangle earrings • For each earring: Open a jump ring **(Basics)** and attach a long rectangle and a short rectangle. Close the jump ring.

2

Open the loop of an earring wire and attach the dangle. Close the loop.

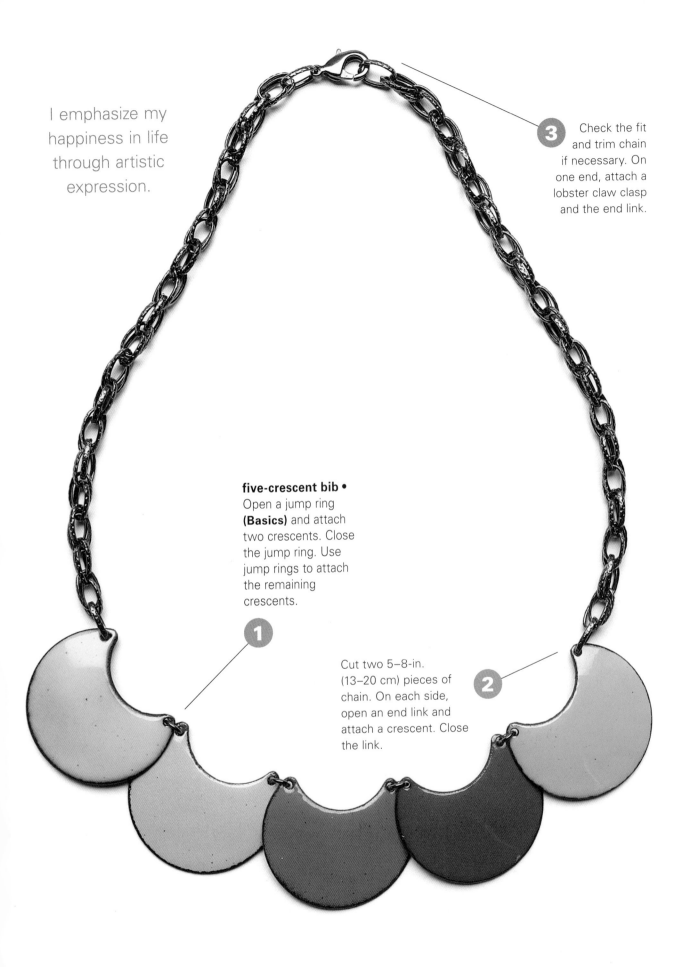

I emphasize my happiness in life through artistic expression.

five-crescent bib •
Open a jump ring **(Basics)** and attach two crescents. Close the jump ring. Use jump rings to attach the remaining crescents.

1

Cut two 5–8-in. (13–20 cm) pieces of chain. On each side, open an end link and attach a crescent. Close the link.

2

Check the fit and trim chain if necessary. On one end, attach a lobster claw clasp and the end link.

3

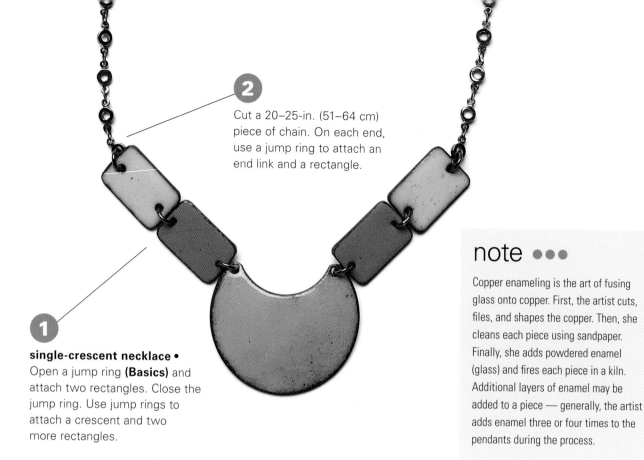

2 Cut a 20–25-in. (51–64 cm) piece of chain. On each end, use a jump ring to attach an end link and a rectangle.

1

single-crescent necklace • Open a jump ring **(Basics)** and attach two rectangles. Close the jump ring. Use jump rings to attach a crescent and two more rectangles.

note •••

Copper enameling is the art of fusing glass onto copper. First, the artist cuts, files, and shapes the copper. Then, she cleans each piece using sandpaper. Finally, she adds powdered enamel (glass) and fires each piece in a kiln. Additional layers of enamel may be added to a piece — generally, the artist adds enamel three or four times to the pendants during the process.

single-rectangle earrings • For each earring: Cut a 1½-in. (3.8 cm) piece of chain. Open a 6 mm jump ring **(Basics)** and attach an end link and a rectangle. Close the jump ring.

1

2 Use a 4 mm jump ring to attach the dangle and the loop of a lever-back earring wire.

materials

crescent earrings
- 2 38 mm enameled crescents
- 3 in. (7.6 cm) chain, 2 mm links
- 4 4 mm jump rings
- pair of earring wires
- 2 pairs of pliers
- diagonal wire cutters

double-rectangle earrings
- 2 38 mm enameled rectangles
- 2 18 mm enameled rectangles, with two holes
- 2 6 mm jump rings
- pair of earring wires
- 2 pairs of pliers
- diagonal wire cutters

five-crescent bib 18 in. (46 cm)
- 5 38 mm enameled crescents, with two holes
- 10–16 in. (25–41 cm) chain, 6–8 mm links
- 4 6 mm jump rings
- lobster claw clasp
- 2 pairs of pliers
- diagonal wire cutters

single-crescent necklace 28 in. (71 cm)
- 38 mm enameled crescent, with two holes
- 4 18 mm enameled rectangles, with two holes
- 20–25 in. (51–64 cm) chain, 2–4 mm links
- 6 6 mm jump rings
- 2 pairs of pliers
- diagonal wire cutters

single-rectangle earrings
- 2 38 mm enameled rectangles
- 3 in. (7.6 cm) chain, 2 mm links
- 2 6 mm jump rings
- 2 4 mm jump rings
- pair of lever-back earring wires
- 2 pairs of pliers
- diagonal wire cutters

Enameled pendants by Marian Stonacek from Happy Mango Beads, happymangobeads.com.

Bohemian blooms

necklace & earrings

This set includes some of **Irina Miech's** favorite design themes — Art Nouveau and steampunk. Stylized pod shapes, ornate leaves, and swinging dangles give the necklace a vintage yet organic feel. The ribbon colors add to the floral feeling, and asymmetry gives the overall look a casual vibe.

1

2

3a

3b

4

1 long dangle • Open a 5 mm jump ring **(Basics)**. Attach a leaf charm and another 5 mm jump ring. Close the jump ring.

2 On a headpin, string: bicone crystal, 5 mm bead cap, 12 mm round bead, 18 mm bead cap, 4 mm spacer, 8 mm bead cap, 5 mm. Make a wrapped loop **(Basics)**.

3a Use two 5 mm jump rings to attach the headpin unit and a 10 mm jump ring. Use a 5 mm jump ring to attach a branch link.

b Attach two more 5 mm jump rings and the branch link.

4 Use an 8 mm jump ring to attach the branch dangle and the leaf charm dangle.

1

2

3

1 short dangles • On a headpin, string a 9 mm bead cap, a 13 mm round bead, and a 9 mm bead cap. Make a wrapped loop **(Basics)**.

2 Cut a ½-in. (1.3 cm) piece of chain. Use a 5 mm jump ring to attach the headpin unit and an end link of chain. Attach an 8 mm jump ring and the other end link.

3 Cut a 1-in. (2.5 cm) piece of chain. Use a 5 mm jump ring to attach a key charm and an end link. Attach an 8 mm jump ring and the other end link.

This jewelry brings together motifs that are close to my heart, evoking images of a secret key opening a wrought iron gate that leads to a beautiful garden.

materials

necklace 26 in. (66 cm)
- 13 mm round bead
- 12 mm round bead
- 4 mm bicone crystal
- 35 mm branch link
- 30 mm key charm
- 22 mm ring
- 20 mm filigree leaf charm
- 18 mm magnolia leaf bead cap
- **2** 9 mm bead caps
- 8 mm bead cap
- **2** 5 mm bead caps
- 4 mm spacer
- 1½ in. (3.8 cm) chain, 4 mm links
- 2½-in. (6.4 cm) headpin
- 10 mm jump ring
- **3** 8 mm jump rings
- **9** 5 mm jump rings
- 36-in. (.9 m) ribbon
- chainnose and roundnose pliers
- diagonal wire cutters

earrings
- **2** 12 mm round beads
- **2** 4 mm bicone crystals
- **2** 4 mm spacers
- **2** 18 mm magnolia leaf bead caps
- **2** 8 mm bead caps
- **4** 5 mm bead caps
- **2** 2½-in. (6.4 cm) headpins
- **2** 10 mm jump rings
- **10** 5 mm jump rings
- pair of earring wires
- chainnose and roundnose pliers
- diagonal wire cutters

Supplies from Eclectica, eclectica beads.com.

1 **necklace** • Make the dangles (p. 126). Open the 8 mm jump rings. Attach the dangles and a 22 mm ring. Close the jump rings.

2 Make a lark's head knot around the ring (**Basics**).

3 With both ends of the ribbon, tie an overhand knot (**Basics**). To wear, slip the ribbon over your head.

Open two 5 mm jump rings (**Basics**). Attach a headpin unit and a 10 mm jump ring. Close the jump rings. Attach two more 5 mm jump rings.

Use a 5 mm jump ring to attach a dangle and the loop of an earring wire.

earrings • For each earring: Make a headpin unit as in step 2 of the long dangle.

Design alternative

Irina made these metal clay charms using leaves to texturize the clay and a natural pod to mold this swirly silver dangle.

A splash of color
necklace

A strand of jewel-toned crackle agate is **Suzann Sladcik Wilson's** quartz of choice for a bright accent piece. This necklace will not only perk up your wardrobe staples like gray, brown, and black, but it'll lift your spirits as well.

Design alternatives

String a pair of top-drilled beads, or choose crystals in a matching color for a lightweight option.

1 **necklace •** Cut a piece of beading wire **(Basics)**. Center a bead on the wire.

2 On each end, string beads until the strand is within 1 in. (2.5 cm) of the finished length.

3 On one end, string a crimp bead and a lobster claw clasp. Repeat on the other end, substituting a jump ring for the clasp. Check the fit, and add or remove beads if necessary on each end. Go back through the last few beads strung and tighten the wire. Crimp the crimp bead **(Basics)** and trim the excess wire.

materials

necklace 18 in. (46 cm)

- 16-in. (41 cm) strand 25 mm nuggets, top drilled
- flexible beading wire, .018 or .019
- 2 crimp beads
- lobster claw clasp and soldered jump ring
- chainnose or crimping pliers
- diagonal wire cutters

Crackle agate nuggets from Beadphoria Boutique, beadphoria.com.

tip

Before you start stringing, set aside two beads with large holes to use on the ends of your necklace.

Bead bold
necklace & earrings

Forest green and peach together? **Cathy Jakicic** wouldn't have thought so, either. But when she saw the strands next to each other, she couldn't deny the attraction. The match needed a little help to find harmony: Czech glass and raku beads that have touches of both colors bridge the gap.

tips ●●●

- The different copper tones in the chain, spacers, and clasp harmonize with the dark rust of the raku and lighter rose tones in the pearls.
- Place smaller beads and spacers evenly on each side to balance and unify both strands.

- Since the sides are not identical, to position the raku bead in the center, you may need to adjust the number of rondelles.
- The raku includes the colors of all the other beads.

- The Czech glass rondelles are similar to the green pearls in color but closer to the light peach in intensity.
- Balance the color blocks between strands by positioning them on opposite sides.

6 On each end, use a jump ring to attach half of a clasp and the link.

5 Cut a 17–19-in. (43–48 cm) piece of 10 mm chain, removing the connectors from both ends. On each end, between the beaded strands, use a jump ring to attach the end link and the link from step 4.

4 Cut two links of 10 mm chain, removing the connectors. On each end of each strand, string three rondelles and a crimp bead. On one side, over both ends, string a 10 mm link and go back through the beads just strung. Repeat on the other end. Crimp the crimp beads **(Basics)** and trim the excess wire.

2 Cut a 1½-in. (3.8 cm) piece of cable chain. Center a pendant on the cable chain. Cut a 24–26-in. (61–66 cm) piece of beading wire. String each end link of cable chain.

3 Cut a three-link piece of 10 mm link chain. Remove the connector from each end. Open a jump ring **(Basics)**. Attach the 10 mm chain and a link of cable chain. Close the jump ring. On each end of the wire, string beads until the strand is within 2 in. (5 cm) of the finished length.

1 **necklace •** Cut a 22–24-in. (56–61 cm) piece of beading wire. Center: spacer, rondelle, 8 mm raku bead, rondelle, spacer. On each end, string beads until the strand is within 2 in. (5 cm) of the finished length.

Mixing the copper tones in the findings adds unity and depth to the multihued design.

Design alternative

For a simpler, lighter look, make a single-strand necklace with just a few pearls.

materials

necklace 16–18 in. (41–46 cm)
- ◆ 50 mm raku teardrop pendant
- ◆ 15-in. (38 cm) strand 18 mm coin pearls, forest green
- ◆ 15-in. (38 cm) strand 18 mm coin pearls, peach
- ◆ **2** 18 mm square raku beads
- ◆ **12** 8 mm square raku beads
- ◆ **20–25** 6 mm wavy spacers
- ◆ **20–25** 4 mm Czech glass rondelles
- ◆ flexible beading wire, .014 or .015
- ◆ 20 in. (51 cm) chain, 10 mm links
- ◆ 1½ in. (3.8 cm) cable chain, 4 mm links
- ◆ **5** 7 mm jump rings
- ◆ **4** crimp beads
- ◆ toggle clasp
- ◆ two pairs of chainnose pliers
- ◆ diagonal wire cutters
- ◆ crimping pliers (optional)

earrings
- ◆ **2** 18 mm coin pearls
- ◆ **2** 8 mm square raku beads
- ◆ **2** 4 mm Czech glass rondelles
- ◆ **2** 10 mm chain links, with one connector attached
- ◆ **2** 2-in. (5 cm) headpins
- ◆ pair of earring wires
- ◆ chainnose and roundnose pliers
- ◆ diagonal wire cutters

Raku beads and pendant from XAZ Bead Company, xazbead.com. Pearls from Pearl Concepts, pearlconcepts.com. Chain from Margola Corp., margola.net. Clasp from Tierra Cast.

1

1 earrings • For each earring: On a headpin, string a pearl, a raku bead, and a rondelle. Make the first half of a wrapped loop **(Basics)**.

2

2 Attach the bead unit and a link. Complete the wraps. Open the loop of an earring wire **(Basics)** and attach the link. Close the loop.

Charmed life

necklace

Growing up with an electrician father, **Ashley Bunting** was always digging through boxes of scrap wire, metal bolts, and bits — and her grandfather's workshop inspired this mixed-material piece. Leave the locket empty so you can add to the piece as you wear it.

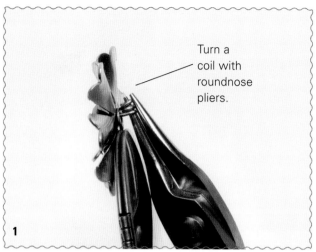

Turn a coil with roundnose pliers.

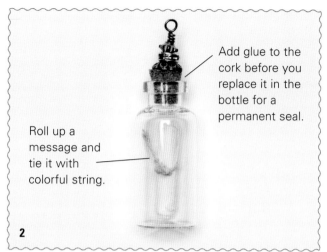

Add glue to the cork before you replace it in the bottle for a permanent seal.

Roll up a message and tie it with colorful string.

1 **necklace •** To make the locket component: On a headpin, string a rondelle, a mini heart clover, a 30 mm carnation, and a locket. Make a coil.

Repeat for the other components (Flower components, below). For components with buttons, open the loop of an eye pin and attach the button. Close the loop. String the remaining layers and make a coil.

2 Remove the cork from a glass bottle. From the bottom, push a headpin through the cork. String a bead cap, a crystal-accent rondelle, and a spacer. Make a wrapped loop **(Basics)**. Write a note, place it in the bottle, and replace the cork.

flower components

gunmetal flower
- 4 mm rondelle
- two 22 mm four-prong stamen flowers
- 35 mm spike banded flower

pink button flower
- **18** mm pink Lucite button
- 35 mm spike banded flower
- 31 mm Lucite impatiens

vinyl flower
- 16 mm Lucite button
- two 22 mm four-prong stamen flowers
- 31 mm Lucite impatiens
- 38 mm brushed cutout flower
- 40 mm vinyl flower

silver flower
- 4 mm rondelle
- 12 mm mini clover
- 35 mm spike banded flower

Jewelry is precious; it can remind us of a place, a time, or a person. It is a tiny object that expresses who we are.

tips ●●●

- Omit the glue on the cork if you want the option of reading the message later.
- If your chain has unsoldered links, open them like jump rings instead of cutting them. That way, you won't waste links.

materials

necklace 21 in. (53 cm)

- 54 mm locket
- 52 mm anchor charm
- 40 mm vinyl flower
- 40 mm glass bottle with cork
- 38 mm brushed cutout flower
- **3** 35 mm spike banded flowers
- **2** 31 mm Lucite impatiens
- 30 mm carnation
- **4** 22 mm four-prong stamen flowers
- 18 mm Lucite button with shank
- **2** 16 mm Lucite buttons with shanks
- 14 mm mini heart clover
- 12 mm mini clover
- 6 mm crystal-accent rondelle
- 6 mm bead cap
- 5 mm spacer
- **2** 4 mm crystal rondelles
- 22–24 in. (56–61 cm) cable chain, 6 mm links
- **11** 7 mm jump rings
- **6** 2-in. (5 cm) headpins
- **2** 2-in. (5 cm) eye pins
- scrap of paper (for message in bottle)
- 2 in. (5 cm) string
- chainnose and roundnose pliers
- diagonal wire cutters
- craft glue (optional)

Supplies from The Beadin' Path, beadinpath.com.

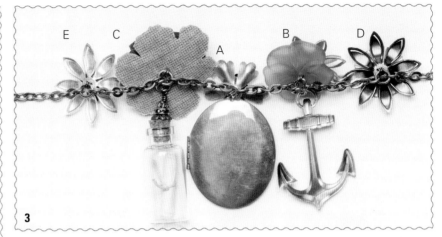

3 Cut two seven-link pieces, two nine-link pieces, an 8–9-in. (20–23 cm) piece, and a 9–10-in. (23–25 cm) piece of chain. Open a jump ring **(Basics)** and attach the coil of the locket component and an end link of each seven-link chain (A). Close the jump ring.

On one end, use a jump ring to attach the end of a seven-link chain, the pink button flower, and an end link of a nine-link chain (B). Repeat on the other end, substituting the vinyl flower (C) for the button flower.

On one end, use a jump ring to attach the end of the nine-link chain, a gunmetal flower, and an 8–9-in. (20–23 cm) chain (D). Repeat on the other end with the silver flower and a 9–10-in. (23–25 cm) chain (E).

Use jump rings to attach the glass bottle and the anchor charm, and to connect the flower components to each other.

4 Use a jump ring to attach a 16 mm button to the end of the 8–9-in. (20–23 cm) chain.

5 Use a jump ring to attach links to form a 1-in. (2.5 cm) loop on the end of the 9–10-in. (23–25 cm) chain.

notes ●●●

You won't want your personal statement necklace to look exactly like mine, but definitely use my techniques for mixing materials to create your own piece. My necklace isn't symmetrical, but here's how I created balance:

- There are Lucite flowers, charms, and buttons on each side, but the larger button is on the same side as the lighter weight charm.
- The light green string on one side echoes the color of the Lucite flower on the other.
- The larger vinyl flower is on the opposite side of the brighter Lucite components to balance the visual impact.
- Gunmetal components are distributed throughout.

tip ●●●

Yes, the locket is backwards! The layered flowers would've kept it from opening out, so I flipped it.

crystal and glass

Czech fire polished

bicone

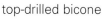

top-drilled bicone

cube

oval

drop

briolette

cone

round

saucer

top-drilled saucer
(with jump ring)

flat back

dichroic

lampworked

glass flowers

leaves

dagger

teardrop

fringe drops

seed beads

triangle

bugle

gemstone shapes

lentil

rondelle

faceted rondelle

round

oval

marquise

rectangle

tube

briolette

teardrop

chips

nugget

pearls, shells, and miscellaneous

go go

round

teardrop

potato

button

stick

petal

keshi

rice

coin

Lucite flowers

donut

shell

bone

horn

heishi

findings, spacers, and connectors

French hook
ear wires

post earring and
ear nut

hoop earring

lever-back
earring

ear
thread

magnetic
clasp

S-hook
clasp

lobster claw
clasp

toggle
clasp

two-strand
toggle clasp

box
clasp

slide clasp

hook-and-eye
clasps

snap
clasp

pinch crimp
end

crimp ends

coil end

crimp cone

tube bail with
loop

tube-shaped and
round crimp beads

crimp
covers

bead tips

jump rings and
soldered jump rings

split ring

spacers

bead caps

pinch bail

multistrand
spacer bars

two-strand
curved tube

single-strand
tube

3-to-1 and 2-to-1
connectors

chandelier
component

bail

cone

stringing tools, materials, and chain

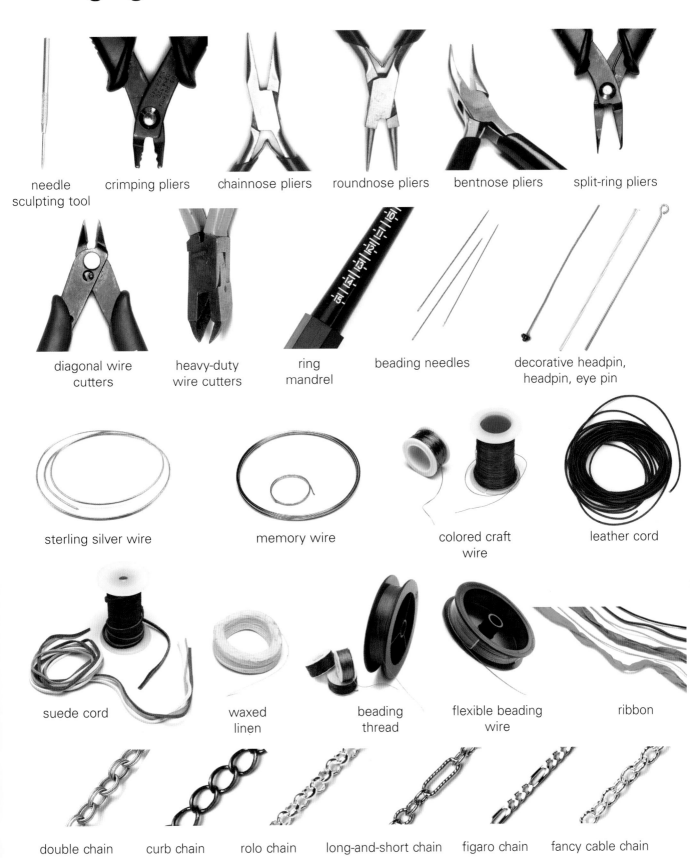

needle sculpting tool

crimping pliers

chainnose pliers

roundnose pliers

bentnose pliers

split-ring pliers

diagonal wire cutters

heavy-duty wire cutters

ring mandrel

beading needles

decorative headpin, headpin, eye pin

sterling silver wire

memory wire

colored craft wire

leather cord

suede cord

waxed linen

beading thread

flexible beading wire

ribbon

double chain

curb chain

rolo chain

long-and-short chain

figaro chain

fancy cable chain

BASICS

plain loop

1

2

3

4

Trim the wire or headpin ³/₈ in. (1 cm) above the top bead. Make a right-angle bend close to the bead.

Grab the wire's tip with roundnose pliers. The tip of the wire should be flush with the pliers. Roll the wire to form a half circle. Release the wire.

Reposition the pliers in the loop and continue rolling.

The finished loop should form a centered circle above the bead.

wrapped loop

1

2

3

4

Make sure you have at least 1¼ in. (3.2 cm) of wire above the bead. With the tip of your chainnose pliers, grasp the wire directly above the bead. Bend the wire (above the pliers) into a right angle.

Using roundnose pliers, position the jaws in the bend.

Bring the wire over the top jaw of the roundnose pliers.

Reposition the pliers' lower jaw snugly into the loop. Curve the wire downward around the roundnose pliers. This is the first half of a wrapped loop.

5

6

opening and closing loops or jump rings

1

2

Position the chainnose pliers' jaws across the loop.

Wrap the wire tail around the wire stem, covering the stem between the loop and the top bead. Trim the excess wire and press the cut end close to the wraps with chainnose pliers.

Hold the loop or jump ring with two pairs of chainnose pliers or chainnose and roundnose pliers, as shown.

To open the loop or jump ring, bring one pair of pliers toward you and push the other pair away. String materials on the open loop or jump ring. Reverse the steps to close the open loop or jump ring.

overhand knot

Make a loop and pass the working end through it. Pull the ends to tighten the knot.

surgeon's knot

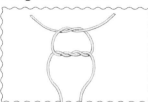

Cross the right end over the left end and go through the loop. Go through again. Pull the ends to tighten. Cross the left end over the right end and go through once. Pull the ends to tighten.

lark's head knot

Fold a cord in half and lay it behind a ring, loop, etc. with the fold pointing down. Bring the ends through the ring from back to front, and then through the fold and tighten.

making wraps above a top-drilled bead

1

Center a top-drilled bead on a 3-in. (7.6 cm) piece of wire. Bend each wire upward to form a squared-off "U" shape.

2

Cross the wires into an "X" above the bead.

3

Using chainnose pliers, make a small bend in each wire to form a right angle.

4

Wrap the horizontal wire around the vertical wire as in a wrapped loop. Trim the excess wire.

folded crimp

1

Position the crimp bead in the notch closest to the crimping pliers' handle.

2

Separate the wires and firmly squeeze the crimp.

3

Move the crimp into the notch at the pliers' tip and hold the crimp as shown. Squeeze the crimp bead, folding it in half at the indentation.

4

Test that the folded crimp is secure.

CONTRIBUTORS

Theresa Abelew Theresa Abelew is editorial associate for *Art Jewelry* magazine. Contact Theresa at 2DogStudios@gmail.com.

Adrianna Amato, originally from Chicago, Ill., now finds inspiration from sunny Florida. She attributes her success to her supportive mother, Marisol, and boyfriend, Brandon. Contact her at wearmeoutjewelry@ yahoo.com or via her website, wearmeoutaccessories.com.

Sarah Arnett is a jewelry designer and marketer who lives in Columbus, Ohio, with her partner — in life and business — Andy Magisano, owner of fancybeads.com. Contact Sarah at sarah@fancybeads.com or visit fancybeads.com.

Sondra Barrington is the Sales Manager at Rings & Things in Spokane, Wash. Contact Sondra at sunnybarrington@gmail.com or view more of her work in the design gallery at rings-things.com.

Sharon Borsavage has been beading for six years, but has always been a crafter. She was a proud member of the 2012 Nunn Design Innovation Design Team. Her favorite place to bead is at home in Plymouth, Pa. Contact Sharon at sjbborsavage@ verizon.net or visit livewirejewelry. blogspot.com.

Ashley Bunting is a jewelry designer based in Portland, Maine, who designs jewelry and writes tutorials for beadinpath.com, is a brand ambassador for Xuron Tools, and runs her independent jewelry business, Miss Ashely Kate. She sells her jewelry in an Etsy shop, online from her website, and at regional shows and fairs in the Northeast. She has been published numerous times in *Bead Style* magazine. She teaches

locally and nationally at venues such as Bead Fest. Contact her at missashleykate@gmail.com.

Stephanie Gard Bussis is a mixed-media jewelry artist and a senior member of Nunn Design's Innovation Team. She lives and works in Lake Elmo, Minn. Contact her at maxandlucie@gmail.com or visit maxandlucie.etsy.com or ollapodrida. etsy.com.

Anne Dilker has recently launched her line of Artifacts Jewelry Design Elements and continues to explore the use of textiles, paper, and anodized aluminum in jewelry design. She is the coauthor of an intensive business course for designers of handmade jewelry called Make More Money Making Jewelry. Contact Anne at annedilker@verizon.net, anne@makemoremoney makingjewelry, or via her website, mosshollowpottery.com.

Anna Elizabeth Draeger is a well-known jewelry designer, former associate editor for *Bead&Button* magazine, and the author of *Crystal Brilliance*, *Great Designs for Shaped Beads*, and *Crystal Play*. Since 2009, Anna has been an ambassador for the Create Your Style with Swarovski Elements program, a handpicked worldwide network of designers who are known for their design expertise and passion for teaching. Her website is originaldesignsbyanna. squarespace.com.

Christi Friesen is the author of nine books, with projects including polymer clay birds, cats, and dragons. See more of her projects, books, and classes at christifriesen.com.

Naomi Fujimoto is editor of *Bead Style* magazine and author of *Cool Jewels: Beading Projects for Teens*.

Visit her at cooljewelsbynaomi.etsy. com, or contact her in care of *Bead Style*.

Monica Han is an award-winning mixed-media jewelry designer and teacher in Potomac, Md. Contact her via email at mhan@dreambeads.biz.

Karen Harris is a security officer from Russellville, Ark., where she lives with her husband and her two daughters. Contact Karen at kaharris39@hotmail.com.

Catherine Hodge designs jewelry in her Michigan studio. She can be contacted at catherinemarissa@ yahoo.com or via her shop, CatherineMarissa.etsy.com.

Gay Isber is a full-time product designer with studios in Austin, Texas, and Raleigh, N.C. Feel free to contact Gay at gayisber@gmail.com or visit gayisber.com.

Cathy Jakicic is the former editor of *Bead Style* magazine and the author of the books *Jewelry Projects from a Beading Insider* and *Hip Handmade Memory Jewelry*. She has been creating jewelry for more than 15 years. Contact her via email at cathyjakicic@att.net.

Brightly colored stones are **Meredith Jensen's** beading material of choice. Her favorite place to buy them: the Bead&Button Show, held each June, just a few miles from her home in Milwaukee. Contact Meredith via her website, m-jewelry.net.

Marcy Kentz lives with her fiancé, Dave, in Berkeley, Calif. They turned their extra room into a studio space. See more of Marcy's designs at marcykentz.etsy.com.

Jane Konkel is a former associate editor of *Bead Style* magazine. Contact her in care of Kalmbach Books.

Kelsey Lawler is assistant editor for *Bead Style* magazine. Contact her at klawler@beadstylemag.com.

Irina Miech is an artist, teacher, and the author of 10 books on jewelry making. She also oversees her retail bead supply business and classroom studio, Eclectica and The Bead Studio, in Brookfield, Wis., where she teaches classes in beading, wirework, and metal clay. Contact Irina at Eclectica, 262-641-0910, or via email at eclecticainfo@sbcglobal.net.

Samantha Mitchell designs jewelry as a way to express her creativity when she's not busy caring for her son. Contact her at samantha@crystylescom, or visit her website, crystyles.com.

As the founder and owner of Nunn Design, **Becky Nunn** believes that everyone is creative and that we are born with natural abilities and a desire to express ourselves in some creative form or another. Contact Becky at becky@nunndesign.com, or visit nunndesign.com.

Sara Oehler is a jewelry designer residing in sunny Phoenix, Ariz. With Jamie Hogsett, she is the author of *Show Your Colors!* She has designed jewelry and written for numerous publications. To ask a beading question, visit softflexcompany.com and click on "Ask Sara."

Madelin Adriani Pratama lives with her husband and two sons in Jakarta, Indonesia. Contact Maddie at madelinadriani@hotmail.com or visit facebook.com/illuminatijuwel.

Carol Ann Reim is a jewelry artist selling in local shops who also specializes in designing custom jewelry, including bridal. Contact her online at carolsepiphany.etsy.com or via email at carolreim.com.

Leslie Rogalski is an artist, jewelry designer, and author. She lives with her husband in Haverton, Pa., and has a daughter studying musical theater. She is a Create Your Style with Swarovski Elements Ambassador and a design team member for Beadalon and John Bead. Contact Leslie at leslierogalski@gmail.com or visit leslierogalski.com.

Leslie Salisbury works as a marketing and graphic designer in Ontario, Canada. She lives with her husband and blended family that includes six kids, a dog, a cat, a bunny, two guinea pigs, and assorted fish. Contact Leslie at craftivity@bell.net or visit craftivityshop.etsy.com.

Brenda Schweder is the author of *Steel Wire Jewelry* and inventor of *Now That's a Jig!*. Contact her via email at b@brendaschweder.com, or visit her website, Now-Thats-a-Jig.com.

Jennifer Short is a full-time symphony musician and a self-taught part-time jewelry designer. She lives in London, Canada, with her musician husband, their super-creative daughter, and two funny, furry shelties. Jennifer can be reached at jensgems@rogers.com.

Arlet Flores Soldevilla was *Bead Style's* Rising Star in the July 2012 issue. Contact Arlet at arletofs@yahoo.com or visit kenasstones.com.

Susan Sudnik lives in Belleair Bluffs, Fla., and co-owns Bead 'n' Sisters with her sisters Jean and Carolyn. She teaches kumihimo and Viking knit. Contact Susan at susansudnik@aol.com or visit beadnsisters.com.

Jill Urquhart's career designing jewelry and instructing bead classes began in 1998 in Clearwater, Fla., after retiring and completing her degree in clothing, textiles, and design. Contact Jill at jurquhart2@tampabay.rr.com.

Ann Westby started making jewelry in 2001 and quickly discovered she had a passion for wirework. She can be contacted via her website, annwestby.com.

Suzann Wilson is the CEO and lead designer of Beadphoria. Contact her at suzann@beadphoria.com or visit beadphoria.com.

Susanne Young lives in Ottawa, Canada, with her furry children, Lola and Jeter. She can be contacted at lolacreations@hotmail.com.

Stitch together
a complete collection!

Focus on learning and perfecting one stitch at a time with the *Stitch Workshop* library! You'll easily create gorgeous projects with help from clear, step-by-step instructions, detailed illustrations, and beautiful, full-color photos.

Stitch Workshop
Peyote Stitch
basic techniques, advanced results

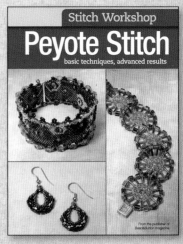

64230 • $17.95

Stitch Workshop
Herringbone Stitch
basic techniques, advanced results

64544 • $17.95

Stitch Workshop
Right-Angle Weave
basic techniques, advanced results

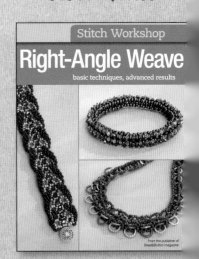

64551 • $17.95

KALMBACH BOOKS

Buy now from your favorite bead or craft shop!
Or at **www.KalmbachStore.com** or call **1-800-533-6644**

Monday – Friday, 8:30 a.m. – 4:30 p.m. CST. Outside the United States and Canada call 262-796-8776, Ext. 661.

P21922

 www.facebook.com/KalmbachJewelryBooks   www.pinterest.com/kalmbachjewelry